T0360860

The Two Sides of Korean Administrative Culture

This book explores two contradictory aspects of Korean culture: competitiveness and collectivism. These two major concepts describe the dynamics of Korean public organizations, which explain the Hangang River Economic Miracle and political democratization. However, not many studies have focused on how competition within the central government, that is, competition among different agencies, has led to an overall competitive government. This book attempts to do so and explains how competition contributed to the rapid economic growth of Korea.

Tobin Im is Professor at the Graduate School of Public Administration, Seoul National University.

Routledge Focus on Public Governance in Asia

Series Editors:
Hong Liu, Nanyang Technological University, Singapore
Wenxuan Yu, Xiamen University, China

Focusing on new governance challenges, practices and experiences in and about a globalizing Asia, particularly East Asia and Southeast Asia, this focus series invites upcoming and established researchers all over the world to succinctly and comprehensively discuss important public administration and policy themes such as government administrative reform, public budgeting reform, government crisis management, public private partnership, science and technology policy, technology-enabled public service delivery, public health and aging, talent management, and anticorruption across Asian countries. The book series presents compact and concise content under 50,000 words long which have significant theoretical contributions to the governance theory with an Asian perspective and practical implications for administration and policy reform and innovation.

Translation and the Sustainable Development Goals
Cultural Contexts in China and Japan
Meng Ji and Chris G. Pope

The Two Sides of Korean Administrative Culture
Competitiveness or Collectivism?
Tobin Im

For more information about this series, please visit https://www.routledge.com/Routledge-Focus-on-Public-Governance-in-Asia/book-series/RFPGA

The Two Sides of Korean Administrative Culture
Competitiveness or Collectivism?

Tobin Im

Routledge
Taylor & Francis Group

LONDON AND NEW YORK

First published 2019
by Routledge
2 Park Square, Milton Park, Abingdon, Oxon OX14 4RN

and by Routledge
52 Vanderbilt Avenue, New York, NY 10017

Routledge is an imprint of the Taylor & Francis Group, an informa business

The author(s) disclosed receipt of the following financial support for the research, authorship, and/or publication of this book: This study was supported by a National Research Foundation of Korea grant from the Korean Government (NRF-2017S1A3A2065838).

British Library Cataloguing-in-Publication Data
A catalogue record for this book is available from the British Library

Library of Congress Cataloging-in-Publication Data
Names: Im, Tobin, author.
Title: The two sides of Korean administrative culture: competitiveness or collectivism? / by Tobin Im.
Description: Abingdon, Oxon; New York, NY: Routledge, 2019. | Series: Routledge focus on public governance in Asia | Includes bibliographical references and index.
Identifiers: LCCN 2019004636 | ISBN 9780367150136 (hardback) | ISBN 9780429054471 (ebook)
Subjects: LCSH: Public administration—Korea (South) | Economic development—Korea (South) | Competition (Psychology) | Competition—Korea (South) | National characteristics, Korean.
Classification: LCC JQ1725 .I443 2019 | DDC 306.2/4095195—dc23
LC record available at https://lccn.loc.gov/2019004636

ISBN: 978-0-367-15013-6 (hbk)
ISBN: 978-0-429-05447-1 (ebk)

Typeset in Times New Roman
by codeMantra

Contents

Figures

Tables

1   Competition

A novel concept?

This introductory chapter will discuss an underlying mechanism of Korea's rapid economic growth and political miracles in the 1960s–1980s. Competitiveness and collectivism are constructed as new concepts that identify the main sources of these major accomplishments, and these two concepts will be demonstrated through the state's crucial role in managing through postwar adversities. The state's role will be emphasized by the significance of bureaucratic coherence in implementing public projects, along with increasingly important citizen participation since democratization.

Explanatory factors of the Korean Miracle

Many developing countries have long envied Korea for its Miracle on the Han River. *The Miracle on the Han River* refers to the period of rapid economic growth in South Korea following the Korean War (1950–1953), during which South Korea transformed from a developing country to a developed country. Numbers show that Korea's gross domestic product (GDP) has increased 386 times from 4 billion United States Dollars (current USD) in 1960 to USD 1.5 trillion in 2017. GDP per capita has also skyrocketed 188 times from USD 158 in 1960 to USD 29,743 in 2017. The country has radically transformed from a war-ruined country into an economic powerhouse in the last few decades. Its economy grew explosively at a two-digit GDP annual growth rate: for most years from 1966 to 1991, the annual GDP growth rate marked somewhere between 10% and 15%. The country's economy has experienced a major leapfrog from exporting raw silk and iron ore, and making light products such as wigs and textiles in the 1960s to producing consumer electronics, oil tankers, and semiconductors since the 1990s. There are a few descriptive pieces of literature that demonstrate past accomplishments of the Korean economy, but there is no convincing explanation of factors other than leadership as well as the Korean bureaucracy's role in the mobilization of resources (Chibber, 2002: 961). Foreign financial aid has been the greatest part of universally accepted theories of economic development in developing countries, but it has not always helped countries in the desired way.

The so-called Dutch disease[1] and the resource curse or cure[2] are two extreme theories that clearly show the limitation of resource factors. There is at least one important missing factor that encompasses all other variables in previous ideas. Another miracle of Korea that is not as well-known as the economic one is its rapid political democratization. Most developed countries had developed their democracy over hundreds of years. In contrast, the Korean democracy has developed in just three or four decades, which is much shorter than in other countries. The people's aspiration for freedom and democracy under the prolonged authoritarian dictatorship from Park Chung-hee to Chun Doo-hwan (1961–1987) had grown. The transition to a democratic political system from military government was achieved by numerous anti-government demonstrations and collective actions of the people. Eventually, the direct presidential election which had long been demanded by demonstrators was held in 1987.

This book deploys competitiveness and collectivism to better understand Korean miracles. While competitions are essential traits that may have contributed to such economic growth, their significance has not been discovered yet. Competitiveness and collectivism together will explain the dynamics of Korean public organizations, which include *the Miracle on the Han River* and political democratization. We will shed light on these two major concepts to understand the state having managed through postwar adversities and having mobilized appropriate resources at proper times. State have also accommodated bureaucratic coherence in implementing these public projects and later kindled increasingly important citizen participation upon democratization.

Before discussing how competitiveness and collectivism have affected the economic growth, this chapter will briefly review previous ideas about economic growth in most developing countries. Then the chapter will proceed to key psychological variables of our interest. While the discussion will not nullify prevalent ideas from existing literature, it will provide a more wholistic perspective on Korean society and its constituents. Researchers in economics and sociology have already developed economic factors as well as cultural and institutional factors, but adding psychological factors as moderating variables will enrich their explanations on economic achievements.

Competitiveness and collectivism may also be independent variables that directly affect the economic growth. Later chapters that explore theoretical backgrounds of competitiveness and collectivism will also elaborate on this potential causal relationship.

Conventional explanations on economic development

Not many pieces of literature have discovered the underlying mechanism of Korea's rapid economic growth. Extant explanations from various academic disciplines largely remain insufficient to the extent that many of them simply describe development processes or suggest economic and demographic variables as major contributing factors. Therefore, most economic development research articles, not specifically focusing on Korean cases, have appeared in economics and sociology academic journals. Lucas (1988), an economist, proposed neoclassical econometric models involving physical capital accumulation, technology changes, and human capital accumulations to explain economic developments in different countries. Lucas adopted the neoclassical economic growth view of Robert Solow and Edward Denison.

Some research, however, such as Granato et al. (1996) and Swank (1996), has suggested culture and institutions as potential explanatory variables of economic growth. Granato et al. (1996) associated with Weber's Protestant cultural attitudes on economic achievement and thrift with positive economic growth. Also included in the analysis were postmaterialist[3] values negatively associated with economic growth, and these cultural values had been listed in the World Values Survey that asked the public which social qualities are important for their children (Granato et al., 1996: 611). The authors specifically mention McClelland's works on achievement motivation that had been indirectly identified throughout the culture via storybooks and schoolbooks for children (Granato et al., 1996: 610). The achievement motivation turned out to be positively associated with the economic growth rate (1960–1989), and three East Asian countries, Korea, Japan, and China, were the top countries with the highest economic growth rate and high achievement motivation scores (Granato et al., 1996). While these authors agreed that in the short-term technology, shocks are likely to be the main component of economic growth, they argue that cultural factors and political, economic institutions are critical explanatory variables that may interpret the difference between South and North Korea's economic growth (Granato et al., 1996: 607–608).

Building upon Granato's assertion, Swank found out that the variation of the 30-year growth rates of 25 countries was largely explained by human capital investment along with communitarian polities (Swank, 1996). The communitarian polities, which Swank proposes to include the Confucian statist institution of East Asian countries and Northern Europe's social corporatist structures, tend to praise collective organizations and group membership as facilitating developments in organizations (Swank, 1996: 669). These factors often mitigate rent-seeking behaviors or free-riding problems from individuals' selfish intentions, and they instead promote concertation and consensus within an organization (Swank, 1996: 669–670), making the mobilization of human resources (organization members) more convenient for policy implementers. These findings imply that the cultural and institutional contexts of a country may influence how economic growth can be driven amid more obvious economic input factors.

These researchers have developed discussions on the significance of cultural contexts in a country's economic growth. After discussion, they are now acknowledged about the limitations of focusing on economic variables. However, they have yet to delve into the specific cultural context of a country and the underlying story behind it. Another drawback or disadvantage of these existing sets of literature is that they are mostly elaborated on from the Western, developed-country perspective. The applicability and ubiquity of a theory may or may not transcend national borders, thus making certain social and economic theories inapplicable in developing countries.

This book will add to the variety of possible explanation of Korea's accomplishments by introducing psychological aspects of Korean people as a major contributor. Later parts of this and other chapters will discuss psychological backgrounds of Korean culture quite extensively, and the second half of this book will develop on these ideas by putting greater emphases on internal dynamics of the Korean government.

Leadership matters

While it is now clearer that culture in addition to economic factors is significantly associated with economic growth, the leadership of a country may emerge as another controlling factor in the relationship. Decisions to invest more capital and resources into certain industries or emphasizing the importance of higher education on engineering mostly originated from the leader's vision and mission. The classic example of such leadership is that of President Park Chung-hee in the 1960s and 1970s. The Park Chung-hee regime in Korea succeeded in creating a competitive atmosphere through charismatic leadership and a centralized bureaucracy. It stems from Park Chung-hee's vision of utilitarian and nationalistic philosophy, and his great mission centered on economic growth, both of which had not been defined in previous regimes' governing philosophy. Park's vision and mission resulted in a major turning point in Korean society (Im, 2008).

Once Park Chung-hee's desire for power had been realized through a coup d'état on May 16, 1961, his vision and mission for a stronger national economy began to be executed through numerous projects. Born in a poor family, Park emphasized that people should no longer suffer from hunger and poverty. He was determined to devise ways to achieve economic growth as it seemed to be the only way to nourish everyone in the postwar adversity. While a vast number of pieces of literature point out that the national goal of economic development was the primary means of justifying the coup (Kim, 1993: 147–148; Kim, 2013: 77), growth was pivotal in distributing national income to the people. The national income at that time was just inadequate for everyone to share. Park further stressed the logic that "the ideal democracy is hardly achieved without a stable economy" during his New Year speech in 1962. Park Chung-hee thus prioritized a state-led planned economy over anything else.

However, there were not enough capital or natural resources within the country to establish sustainable and lucrative industries. Park Chung-hee's strategic choices accelerated the economic growth in the 1970s. Importing natural resources was unavoidable to initialize manufacturing industries and power plants, but Park pointed out that efficiency should be the core philosophy in mobilizing resources. As a strategic and rational actor, Park initially adopted the import substitution industrialization strategy. Instead of importing construction materials such as cement or fertilizers for the agricultural industry, he ordered domestic production of these products. When the international political economy changed, he switched to an export-led growth strategy that eventually resulted in *the Miracle on the Han River* (Tadashi, 2008). The strategy required export-led businesses to almost dominate most intermediate and primary resources. With most resources concentrated on these strategic businesses, Korean industries later gained comparative advantage on steel, shipbuilding, and electronics (semiconductors).

Aside from the strategic use of physical resources, Park Chung-hee also pursued efficiency and professionalism in bureaucracy. He emphasized that efficiency in bureaucracy would support his strategic choices; he also replaced corrupt and incompetent officials in numerous government positions with competent personnel from the military (Im, 2008: 224). Whenever military personnel showed their limited administrative capacity, Park implemented a career bureaucracy based on performance rather than a spoils system. He also demanded professionalism in bureaucrats by introducing the civil service system that comes in a package with privileged pension and health care service back in the 1960s. These measures helped to motivate bureaucrats by delegating policy making power to technocrats, which resulted in their full contribution to the economy takeoff.

With a powerful leadership marked by efficiency and professionalism, the Park regime gained its status as the main contributor in Korea's rapid economic growth, despite long controversies on its legitimacy. The president's leadership strengthened bureaucrats' policy implementation power in addition to utilizing local resources, as can be seen in the Saemaul Movement (the 'new town' movement) in the 1960s and 1970s. The coherent decision-implementation process may pertain to dictatorship, as many people have criticized. However, despite severe criticisms on decades of forceful execution of power onto the people and negative side effects, the strong leadership unchecked by opposing powers resulted in a bureaucratic coherence (Chibber, 2002).

As stated earlier, leadership was an important factor, leading to a stunning development in Korea. However, there still remain many questions that leadership studies are not able to answer. For example, it is rarely elaborated how and why national plans initiated by the Park regime survived under different leadership. Because those plans were not highly systemized or institutionalized, they would not have been hard to change. Also, national leaders were likely to abandon the predecessor's plan because they needed to legitimize their presence. Another example of an unanswered question is how national plans and systems formed in the development era have influenced politics and social culture in Korea. In order to deal with these unexplored answers, we need to concentrate on a fundamental mechanism.

Governance from psychocultural perspectives

Governance and competitiveness

Most studies have investigated the governance mechanism based on the power approach: who governs and how they govern. However, only a few studies have explored the governance system with respect to social-cultural aspects. Specifically, studies did not pay attention to the socio-cultural and psychological characteristics of the ruling elite or to those of the people. While Korea's economic growth in the 1960s–1980s, as most other researchers claim, does pertain to the public administration's leadership and its cooperation with the people, the underlying psychology between officials and citizens has not been clearly identified. In this regard, there needs to be a novel approach that can shed new light on the miracles in Korea. This book will dedicate most of its pages to discussions on two psychological factors that have contributed to the growth: competitiveness and collectivism.

Competitiveness and collectivism seem to be contradictory concepts that cannot coexist. However, they have been essential values prevalent in Korean organizations, public or private. These two values have helped organization members to compete within and with other organizations. The initial onset of competitiveness of a person happens when he or she wants to be a better person. On the other hand, this person may compare how much he or she has achieved with where others stand. The first case is personal development competitiveness (PDC), and the latter is hyper-competitiveness (HC). These two values together result in competition among people.

The competitiveness of an organization's member may lead to numerous competitions within an organization, and these competitions can further result in competitions among different organizations. At the point when the intra-organization competition ends, and inter-organization competition begins, the collectivist nature of organizational members is likely to emerge. Once competitors, they may work together in a group to win in a larger competition with other organizations. These contradictory values may appear even in a family, the preliminary form of organization, not to mention their prevalence in schools, private companies, and public organizations. Throughout different levels of competition, adequate government leadership may have affected how people behave.

Back to the Saemaul Movement case, President Park Chung-hee's leadership not only caused bureaucratic coherence but also a competition to better achieve the common goal. Eom (2011) conveys that numerous actors have engaged in Korea's economic development. He has identified the street-level contribution of local bureaucrats, along with citizens' efforts in adapting to bureaucratic endeavors to reform the local economy. The Saemaul Movement (translated 'new-town' movement) in the 1970s, according to Eom's extensive review of extant literature, achieved its goals through more frequent interaction between local bureaucrats and rural residents. These interactions may represent two sides of a coin: positive anecdotes on the Saemaul Movement claiming the bottom-up relationship between local residents and local bureaucrats, and negative stories telling that the bottom-up leadership appeared to suppress the democratic desires of the Korean people.

There may be disagreements over the movement's positive and negative effects on Korean communities, but President Park Chung-hee's leadership seems to have instigated both competition and collectivism in people's attitudes. During the Saemaul Movement, local bureaucrats experienced promotion and pay-raises mostly based on their individual performance on local economy improvements. These bureaucrats had to get into fierce competitions to perform better than their peers while achieving the same national goal: make local (rural) economies better. Some rural residents, in association with local officials, were awarded prizes when their village successfully performed better than their neighboring villages. Major projects included house roof improvements and road improvements, both of which were intended to redesign and renovate rural areas into more visually attractive ones. People tried to do better than others, but it is important to notice that these competitions were still based on the collectivist nature inherent in Korean communities.

Aside from economic developments and local developments marked by *the Miracle on the Han River* and the Saemaul Movement, Korea has also exhibited miraculous developments in its democracy. In 1987, the democratic movements involved major radical reforms in the Korean government. These movements successfully replaced the authoritarian regime with a democratic one. The spirit of these movements, often motivated by calls for equality and justice, has further extended its influences in decentralization and the impeachment of presidents. It can also be explained, at least partially, by the competitiveness and collectivism that have persisted through Korean history.

What is expected from this book?

This book will help practitioners of developing countries utilize the competitiveness trait in human resource management, education, and civil service exams. Audiences from developed countries may also obtain insights for their research on economic developments around the world.

This book consists of two parts. Part I discusses psychological and individual dimensions of competitiveness. Part II deals with organizational and sociological aspects of competitiveness. Part I consists of three chapters, including this introductory part to the book. Starting with Chapter 2, the author begins a detailed discussion on competitiveness. The first type to be discussed is competitiveness at the individual level. The author coins "fatalism" as a widespread notion in many developing countries. The Korean War had frustrated the Korean people, but their desires for a better life plus pursuits of egalitarianism and superiority resulted in everlasting efforts to be winners in the competition. These ambitions have resulted in cultural phenomena including, but not limited to, enthusiastic races to top colleges and a "taste for haste".

In Chapter 3, the author further develops the concept of competitiveness at the individual level. He first provides different conceptual frameworks of intra-organizational competitiveness, then identifies the family as a preliminary source of competition among organization members. Fighting for more or at least an equal portion of limited family resources led to the concentration of resources to the best-performing child in the family. The same has often happened in different levels of organizations: at school, at work, and even in public organizations. Although the best-performing members help enhance the overall performance of an organization, desire for a better position within an organization keeps people competing with each other.

Chapter 4 explains the theories and concepts of inter-organizational competitiveness. In particular, the author first introduces general theories regarding why competition is inherent in a bureaucracy. Theories will be followed by Korean examples of ministry egoism and ministry sectionalism, all of which depict apparent bureaucratic competition. Case studies involve power struggles among Korean central government agencies for policy jurisdiction. Examples will also extend to competition among local governments over major public projects.

Chapter 5 emphasizes the role of a government to instigate competition between members of a society. The regionalism that has divided the Korean political landscape since the 1960s plays a determinant role in conflict generating as well as political development. In this framework, the Korean government not only took initiatives in policy areas by direct intervention but also encouraged competition-friendly atmospheres throughout its political groups. Such actions differ from more traditional institution-building activities of a government.

The author concludes the book with Chapter 6. This chapter is intended to serve as a catalyst to redefining competitiveness and competition for the future. Korean cases have shown that competition has become fierce in many areas of society. Beyond-optimal level of competition has led to social stress and even inefficiencies. Competition has often destroyed the social capital: from families, which have been said to be the most preliminary sources of competition, to friendships, entrepreneurs, and governments. The author stresses the need for the optimal level of competition.

Notes

1 Dutch disease was first coined in 1977 in the Economist. The term describes the decline of the manufacturing sector in the Netherlands after discovering a large natural gas field in 1959 (Lee, 2015: 2).

2 Resource curse depicts situations mostly in middle- and low-income countries where plentiful resources do not guarantee economic growth but instead result in economic adversities (Ross, 1999; Goodman & Worth, 2008).

3 Postmaterialism is a "value orientation that emphasizes self-expression and quality of life over economic and physical security". The term was first coined by Ronald Inglehart in his book *The Silent Revolution: Changing Values and Political Styles among Western Publics* (1977) (Excerpt from Encyclopedia Britannica, retrieved September 16, 2018).

References

Chibber, V. (2002). Bureaucratic rationality and the developmental state. *American Journal of Sociology*, 107(4), 951–989.

Eom, S. (2011). Between mobilization and participation: A study on the roles of public officials in local administrations during the rural Saemaul Undong in the 1970s. *Korean Public Administration Review*, 45(3), 97–122.

Goodman, J., & Worth, D. (2008). The minerals boom and Australia's 'resource curse.' *Journal of Australian Political Economy*, 61, 201–219.

Granato, J., Inglehart, R., & Leblang, D. (1996). The effect of cultural values on economic development: Theory, hypotheses, and some empirical tests. *American Journal of Political Science*, 40(3), 607–631.

Im, T. (2008). How has administrative philosophy changed in Korea? A historical approach to governing philosophies appearing over the last 60 years (in Korean). *Korean Journal of Public Administration*, 46(1), 211–251.

Kim, D. (1993). Feature: 30 Years of Military Government – Dissection of Park Chung-hee era, A Modern analysis on the Economic Development Policy of Park Chung-hee.

Kim, J. (2013). The rise of the Seonjinguk discourse and the formation of developmental national identity during the Park Chung-Hee Era: Analyzing presidential addresses and the Chosun Ilbo. *Korean Journal of Sociology*, 47(1), 71–106.

Lee, S. (2015). The Impact of Official Development Assistance on Government Effectiveness: From the Perspective of Government Competitiveness (unpublished doctoral dissertation). Seoul National University, Seoul, Korea.

Lucas, R. Jr. (1988). On the mechanics of economic development. *Journal of Monetary Economics*, 22, 3–42.

Ross, M. L. (1999). The political economy of the resource curse. *World Politics*, 51(2), 297–322.

Swank, D. (1996). Culture, institutions, and economic growth: theory, recent evidence, and the role of communitarian polities. *American Journal of Political Science*, 40(3), 660–679.

Tadashi, K. (2008). *The Policy Choice of the Park Chung-hee Government.* Seoul: Humanitas (in Korean).

2 Competition traits as psychological drivers

What made South Korea more successful than other developing countries? Many experts and scholars in diverse fields have identified various determinants of economic growth. This chapter attempts to find other pieces of evidence from a number of competition traits that are deeply ingrained throughout Korean society. Such traits have been at the core of both economic and social developments in Korea, and thus people have long been exposed to competitive environments. Most of these exposures attain to the government's efforts in pushing the rapid economic growth. As a result, Korea has overcome economic adversity in a short period of time. It has successfully changed its status as a foreign aid recipient country to a donor country, having overcome challenges through different competitions within. We classify Korean's unique psychological characteristic as '*uliseong*', family-like collectivism, and '*chemeyeon*', a 'social face', and explain how these inherited cultural-psychological characteristics affect personal and organization.

Fatalism: the common context in developing countries

Developing countries are generally stranded and hopeless. They usually do not have goals and easily adapts to the current situation. It has been often argued that a common characteristic of underdeveloped and developing countries is a deep-rooted fatalism[1] amyaong the people living with a 'give up and give in' mentality. Fatalistic and passive attitudes toward life are the biggest barrier to social change and economic development as people believe that they are not able to change the situation itself (Paik, 1978).

Specifically, fatalistic individuals are oriented to the past, so they tend to look back at the '*good old days*'. They also view change as burdensome, exacerbating the confusion in a more unpredictable and uncontrollable way (Lee, 1982). For instance, one of the reasons why the heavy amount of international aid did not lead to substantial economic development is that those who have been inclined to fatalism for a long time think achieving success does not depend on human efforts, but rather on God's will. To make matters worse, the beneficiaries of aid do care about what they have right now, but do not pay attention to how they can survive and thrive without external aid in the long run (e.g. Bista, 1991; Brewer, 2012).

Meanwhile, studies in economic psychology and cross-cultural psychology have found the effect of attitudinal factors such as work ethics, attitudes to competitiveness, money, achievement, etc. on national economic development, such as the level of GDP and annual economic growth rate. In particular, a strong motivation to do better than others is a crucial factor to facilitate economic growth. Not surprisingly, South Korea was a typical example showing that a high level of economic growth driven by people who were oriented to competition (e.g. Furnham et al., 1994; Van de Vliert et al., 2000).

Fatalistic beliefs among people were prevalent in traditional Korean society (Im, 2018: 527). Under a rigid social class system, one's social status was predetermined by her/his family from birth and there was a rare chance to move up in the social hierarchy. Consequently, people of the lower social class learned powerlessness from repetitive experiences through the ages. When encountering difficulties or misfortune, for example, people tended to blame or accept their own '*Palja* or *Unmyong*', which means fate or destiny in Korean. The old Korean adage that "*Even the King cannot save the poor*" also illustrates a hopeless/helpless attitude toward poverty.

Fatalism is another side of a coin of negative attitude toward change. Not having an optimistic view on the future, people refuse to prepare for the future by saving or deterring gratification. The traditional class system drastically changed when the Korean War was over. Above all, through a land reform from 1950 to 1951, the privileged ruling class of landed gentry (*yangban* in Korean) entirely collapsed (Kang, 2011). In addition, the majority of the population were homogenous in their economic status because they suffered from absolute poverty in the aftermath of the war. These imply that everyone had relatively equal opportunities to move upward economically and socially. Moreover, with the motto "*Let's Live Well*", the government highlighted the value of working hard to the people in the process of industrialization. People began to perceive that their success depends on themselves, not on social status or heaven's will (Kim, 1990). In the end, competition derived from the strong willingness of both a person and a society to escape from poverty and to move upward led to economic growth. Increased social mobility created newly emerging social classes based on competition: a middle class and an educated class.

Fatalism can also be explained from a *time* perspective. Time used to be one of the bases for theory in the 1960s introduced by Lee (1966). His "time perspective theory" emphasizes that human performance underlies the time orientation toward the future. This attitude keenly interconnected with goal-oriented behavior. Based on the mode of attitude toward time, Lee classified people into three types: *Developmentalist*, *Escapist*, and *Exploitationist*. *Developmentalist* refers to individuals or groups with positive attitudes toward change who have a strong belief about their time and future. The *Escapist* type is pessimistic individual and group who trusts the past rather than the future. The *Exploitationist* type values the current time. From this perspective, the role of government during the developmental era was transforming Koreans from agricultural to Entrepreneurial. The agricultural trait adapts nature as a gift and aims to live harmoniously. The Entrepreneurial trait views nature as the goal of conquering. Europeans are a good example who already constructed railways and bridges across mountains and rivers. Therefore, the crucial role of government was to help people shift their mindset from agricultural oriented to Entrepreneurial oriented to admire the future and change.

The concept of competitiveness: *envy vs motivation?*

Are Koreans born to be competitive? *"A hungry stomach is better than an aching stomach"* is just one example among numerous Korean proverbs related with enviousness. Aching stomach implies one having digestive problems. It depicts an envious situation that if someone succeeds, one cannot celebrate together because he or she cannot eat well and will have an uncomfortable digestion. Whether we call this sort of emotion 'jealousy', 'rivalry', or 'envy', it tells that Korean people have a strong will to be better than others. Although there are complex factors that account for development in Korea, most would agree that a competitive spirit of individuals led to rapid economic growth. And the government also designed policies activating and catering to this spirit. For instance, the government inevitably promoted competition in order to allocate scarce resource efficiently. A competitive person is likely to be motivated where competition is emphasized.

The theoretical basis of competitiveness lies in social comparison theory. Social comparison refers to the degree to which a person evaluates her/his own abilities, values, attitudes, and behaviors with others (Festinger, 1954). Instinctively, people try to find a reference person or group in order to confirm where they are. In the absence of an objective standard, people evaluate themselves by subjectively comparing themselves with others. These attitudes are caused by the fear that a person may lose her/his position in the group where she/he belongs. That is, behaviors of comparing oneself to others can be interpreted as status-seeking behaviors (Garcia et al., 2010).

Some people are competitive by nature while others are vulnerable to stress from competitive environments. This distinctive personal characteristic is known as trait competitiveness. Generally, trait competitiveness is defined as "the desire to excel in comparison to others, and the enjoyment of competition" (Newby & Klein, 2014). According to studies examining the relationship between trait competitiveness and performance, competitive people tend to set higher goals for themselves and exert greater effort to achieve them (e.g. Graziano et al., 1997). Competitive trait is a great concept for understanding how a person becomes highly performant, whether a competitive person was born or not.

Interpersonal competitiveness and goal competitiveness

According to Griffin-Pierson (1990), competition is composed of interpersonal competitiveness (IC) and goal competitiveness. IC is a desire to be better than others, a desire to win in an interpersonal situation, and an attitude of enjoying interpersonal competition. This reflects the traditional view of competition. On the other hand, goal competitiveness is the desire to excel, the desire to achieve the goal, and the desire to do the best that one can.

The factors that affect competition are largely classified into individual factors and situational factors. Situational factors also affect individual factors. Individual factors are further subdivided into personal factors and relational factors. Personality factors include personality variables such as goal orientation characteristics and award oriented characteristics such as scores, grades, performance levels, and promotion.

Yang (2016) suggested that the competitiveness is composed of two dimensions: IC and Personal Development Competitiveness (PDC). IC is a desire to compete to win or win over others. PDC is a desire to do the best that one can do in a competition aiming at self-development, not a victory in competition with others (Figure 2.1).

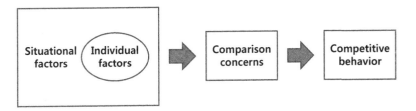

Figure 2.1 Impact factor of competitiveness.
Source: Author's own.

Economic development and increased awareness of equality

During Choson Dynasty Korea, lasting from the 14th to the 20th century, four rather distinct social strata developed: the scholar-officials, collectively referred to as the *yangban*; the *chungin* (literally "middle people"), technicians and administrators subordinate to the *yangban*; the commoners or *sangmin*, a large group composed of farmers, craftsmen, and merchants; and the *ch'ommin* (literally "despised people") at the bottom of society. To ensure stability, the government devised a system of personal tallies in order to identify people according to their status. However, as the economy grew and developed, Confucian oriented culture deeply rooted in Korean mentality was also rapidly replaced by the Western way of thinking. Koreans expressively started to be aware of 'equality'.

After the end of the Korean War, most people had to resume their destroyed lives with a similar resource. In other words, people began to compare their economic and social status with their surroundings. Furthermore, people started to have the desire to be treated equally, especially by 'obtaining opportunities' since 'opportunity' is also a critical 'resource'.

Competition arouses envy because one becomes a loser inevitably in a competitive situation. That is, people feel envy when they want what others have. There are two different types of envy: benign and malicious envy. Benign envy is a positive emotion that motivates people to work hard to catch up with others. Malicious envy works as negative motivation to take away what others have (Smith et al., 2016). As far as there is a realist hope to be a winner, people tend to envy benignly, and vice versa. In this sense, during 1970s and 1980s in Korea, benign envy was the main driver for personal and national development, thanks to the government's efforts for creating social climate toward a rosy future.

Can-do mindset and the government

The role of government was embedding 'can-do mindset' to citizens. 'Can-do mindset' requires a goal, and usually, it is overcoming constraints and becoming better than others. As industrialization driven by the government progressed from the early 1960s, a new social class was created in Korea: the middle class. Many people left the rural areas to get "newly created" jobs in urban areas when plans for industrialization and economic development were initiated. Also, some started their own businesses as the population in urban areas increased. Those who accumulated wealth through hard work in industrial fields or other commercial fields became the middle class (Kim, 1990). In this period, everyone had relatively equal opportunities and the success of those whom she/he did know (e.g. neighbors, kinship) motivated her/him to work.

Until the 1980s, the middle class consisted of diverse groups who were relatively homogenous in terms of economic status. This formation of the middle class in South Korea is different from that of Western countries. In Korea, the middle class was regarded as a by-product of a government-driven development plan because the government needed legitimacy to maintain its authority and justify its existence during the 1970s–1980s. People eagerly wanted economic prosperity. To promote social stability and economic growth, therefore, increasing the middle class was a kind of implicit social contract between the government and the people (Koo, 2018).

Along with a strong desire to move upward in a competitive society, Koreans began to compare themselves with others. People had to prove that they were superior to others. Not to be a loser in competition, at the same time, they kept an eye on how others were treated in a society. In other words, people became sensitive to equal or fair treatment as competition was intense (Im, 2018: 527).

Competition for being an educated class

One can hardly deny that education contributed to economic development in South Korea. The positive relationship between education and economic growth also has been empirically identified. Since South Korea is not a country rich in natural resources (e.g. oil or mineral deposits) national leaders have strongly stressed the importance of human resources to achieve advances in industries and technologies. To satisfy the needs of national development, therefore, the government established a universal public education system in 1948 which impose all children to go to elementary school for six years. As a result, illiteracy rates among population significantly decreased by the 1960s. It is important for national development because education for literacy and numeracy enables people to have abilities to participate socially and economically. Without basic education, it is difficult for individuals to learn higher skills. Furthermore, the rate of secondary-school enrollment and higher education attainment has continuously increased. Higher education directly affected income level: the higher the level of education, the higher level of income (Sorensen, 1994). At the societal level, as the educated group of people increased, national productivity and competitiveness were enhanced along with technological advances in industries.

A good education system itself copied from other countries does not guarantee successful implementation. In Korea, elevating the national education level was possible thanks to rather individual efforts than institutional reforms. A desire of parents to give their children a better education was exceptionally high because the majority of the parent generation had not been educated at all. People who had a secondary education were only 5% of the population in 1945. By supporting higher education, parents wanted their children to have a 'good or better' occupation with higher salaries. Because they had equal access to education, people could fairly compete for the university entrance exam. That is, the 'rags-to-riches' story was realized when a person had a higher education. Regardless of family income status, the chance of getting a job with a higher salary and social status was increased once a person studied at a so-called "good" university. In addition, as their economic needs were met, the middle-class parents who were the economic beneficiaries of industrialization wanted their children to have a socially recognized occupation (Sorensen, 1994), such as judges, prosecutors, professors, or high-rank public officials. These mean that people perceived education as a means for upward social mobility: Higher education became a positional good, which means "one is worse off, in some respect, than one would be if that good were distributed equally" (Brighouse & Swift, 2006).

From the 1960s, the demand of college-educated employees began to rapidly rise in the private sector as South Korea shifted from an agricultural economy to an industrialized economy (e.g. manufacturing, heavy, and chemical industry). While those with lower education levels were hired in labor-intensive jobs, people with degrees began their careers in professional or managerial positions, known as white collar jobs (Sorensen, 1994). There was also a wage gap between the two groups. According to national statistics between 1975 and 1987, the wages of those with a four-year university degree was approximately 2.2 times higher than high school graduates (Lee & Brinton, 1996). As people witnessed and experienced the benefits of higher education, the competition for a university degree got intensified.

Most of those socially respectable professions mentioned previously were concentrated in the public sector since economic development was extensively driven by the government during the early stage of industrialization. Koreans perceived public service as a noble profession because of the Confucian legacy, even though there was no obvious social class in an industrialized society. As a result, the government attracted and hired competent young people who successfully planned and implemented economic development policies. To encourage public employees, the President rapidly promoted those who showed exceptional performance at his discretion. Also, policy elites who had expert knowledge in economic development were appointed as an advisory member in the Blue House (Korean presidential residence). They felt proud of contributing to national growth. To get into these limited positions with social prestige, applicants had to pass the nation-wide exam, which is a highly selective process. In order to pass the exam, one must win over fierce competition among numerous young college graduates.

Today, issues of social polarization caused by quantitative economic development over the previous half-century come to the surface. Some people may strongly disagree that competition led to a high level of economic development in Korea. Nevertheless, it is undeniable that Koreans are still fiercely competitive and enjoy competition. Especially, competitiveness is most evident when it comes to education: Korean parents are notorious for their education fever. The so-called "Republic of examination hell" heavily contributes to internalizing competition. Therefore, Koreans are familiar with competitive situations by being exposed to competition from early stages in life, ultimately forming the unique Korean style of competitiveness.

Excessive competition

There are different aspects of individual competitiveness. Hyper-competitiveness, also known as IC, emphasizes getting power by winning over a competitor. Self-interest is the highest priority for those high in hyper-competitiveness. On the contrary, people with PDC not only put a high value on achievement and self-sufficiency from competition but also care about others' welfare and social values (Ryckman et al., 1997). To a society, PDC is more beneficial and healthier. People respect others' values, goals, experiences, and ideas. Also, they learn from others.

That is, people do not view others as a competitor. Furthermore, they perceive that negative behaviors such as dishonesty, cheating, and manipulation hinder cooperation with others as well as self-development. In a society where interpersonal competition is extremely intense, on the other hand, people are likely to harm or undermine others at any cost. A person regards others as the enemy to beat. In the end, distrust will be widespread among people (Ryckman et al., 1997; Mudrack et al., 2012). For example, those with higher individual development competitiveness are less likely to accept corruption while those with higher IC tolerate corruption when they perceive their organization emphasizes performance superiority (Choi et al., 2018).

These concepts of trait competitiveness developed by Western scholars are fundamentally based on the observations of people living in countries with an individualistic culture. However, collectivism based on family-ties is an inherent part of Korean culture, so Koreans' attitudes toward competition should be differently interpreted. With the cultural aspects of competition, therefore, the following will present how competition and attitudes toward competition work as a driver of Korean development.

Korea is known for its collectivist culture, and in a collective culture, individuals are more tied down for the sake of the groups' interests (Hofstede, 2011). In this regard, Koreans tend to identify themselves within a group where they belong, such as family, school, or workplace. For instance, according to a cross-cultural experiment in the book *"The geography of thought: How Asians and Westerners think differently… and why"* written by Nisbett (2004), when people are asked to introduce themselves, Westerners focus on their individual experiences and stories, while Koreans tend to tell self-stories by focusing on their relationships. These cultural features can explain the way a person behaves toward competition.

Collectivist culture in Korea was derived from familism[2]: one's social identity derived by identifying oneself with their family. In Korean traditional society, more than four generations of extended families settled in one village. Also, extended families had common ownership of land inhered from their ancestors. Therefore, cooperation among family members was inevitably a part of life (Kim, 1990). Although the traditional society collapsed and competition became intense, the certain values embedded in familism were continued. Those who identify themselves as a member of a certain group tend to show a higher commitment to where they belong. They also want their own group to be the best. These cultural characteristics are reflected in the two mechanisms moderating excessive competition: *uliseong* and *chemyeon*.

Uliseong as camaraderie

In many cases, individuals who joined at the same periods do not have equally guaranteed promotion. Also, an employee's competence does not always ensure a timely promotion. For instance, a chief official (a public official of grade 5) beginning a public career at the Ministry of Strategy and Finance (MOSF) has a lower chance of being promoted to a secretary official (a Class 4) than his counterparts in other ministries. In fact, MOSF's attractive *uliseong* and strong identity draw quite a number of applicants, and the applicants generally score higher in the national exam compared to applicants for other departments. Talented and skilled individuals flocking to one specific agency causes a so-called clogging "traffic" in human resource, and is a reason for a delayed promotion of an MOSF civil servant.

In contrast, a new-comer in another ministry, say the Ministry of Environment (ME), is likely to get a promotion earlier than his colleagues at MOSF.[3] MOSF members who fall behind in the promotion race can feel deprived because falling behind sounds unacceptable to those competent workers.

However, a late promotion, or defeat in promotion competition, is offset to some degree by *uliseong* among members of an organization. This is why still many public official candidates aspire to start their career at MOSF. Through *uliseong*, a member expects to have proper compensation afterward, thanks to the organization's reputation. In fact, every ministry of the central government has a unique culture that strengthens a sense of fellowship. Such a distinctive culture sometimes leads to an undesirable phenomenon (e.g. *Gwanpia*[4]), but is also an effective way of delineating organizational identification among members (Table 2.1).

Table 2.1 Number of positions by grade in MOSF and ME, respectively (%), as in December 2016

Grade	1–2	3	4	5	6	7	8	9	*Total*
MOSF[a]	54 (5)	54 (5)	257 (24)	562 (53)	103 (10)	25 (2)	4 (0)	1 (0)	1060 (100)
ME[b]	24 (1)	15 (1)	125 (7)	330 (18)	402 (22)	339 (19)	393 (21)	197 (11)	1825 (100)

Source: Author's calculation from the data of Ministry of Personnel Administration statistics board.

a   MOSF: Ministry of Finance and Strategy.
b   ME: Ministry of Environment.

Uliseong functions as a suppressor of intra-organizational competition, while boosting inter-organizational competition. Because the reputation of an organization, in addition to one's seniority, is the most critical factor of promotion, *uliseong* forms relatively quickly within an elite group, such as the government bureaucracy, compared to the private sector. Most bureaucrats work until their pre-set retirement age; while they are periodically rotated from one position to another within a ministry, they would still have to encounter colleagues throughout their public career. *Uliseong*, then, is the psychological basis for consoling oneself or ostensibly congratulating others' on their promotion when one has failed because one believes – or wants to believe – that the following turn will be his/hers. Thus, people tend to avoid being seen as a competitive person, since such an image of a person would mean an inappropriate lack of *uliseong*. On the other hand, *uliseong* promotes competition when the competitor belongs to an external organization, enhancing inter-organizational competition.

Chemyeon *as saving face in public lives*

Among Confucian societies, Korea is well-known for its culture of collectivism and authoritarianism even during the developmental era. Although sensitivity to face value is common worldwide, it is more important in societies that emphasize humanness, Confucian sense of shame, and *chemyeon*. People restrain themselves from expressing their true emotion such as anger in face of others. Especially losers in a competition do not complain fairness of the game. In the meantime, concealed competition, i.e. pretending to be as calm as if there is no competition, is likely to prevail in the social life. Such cultural features have been more prevalent in the public sector than in its private counterpart (Oh, 2017). Administrative culture in the government bureaucracy is more rigid and authoritarian. Bureaucrats emphasize strict vertical relationships between subordinates and superiors, and they prioritize authority. They also prefer formal and official treatment that matches their ranks, and they tend to identify themselves with their organizations.

In other cases, *chemyeon* mitigates imminent organizational conflicts due to competition. When a junior is promoted to a higher position than the senior in the same department, which occasionally happens, the senior is usually transferred to another department considering the senior's *chemyeon*. This example shows how *chemyeon* mitigates the harsh aftermath of competition. In other words, *chemyeon* can be considered a psychological mechanism that prevents complications from excessive competition within the Korean bureaucracy.

The *chemyeon*-oriented culture also forms a relationship-oriented atmosphere in a workplace. Bureaucrats are often sensitive to peer evaluations regarding work attitudes and reputation. In order to maintain a well-balanced human relationship, bureaucrats show concern not only in task performance but also in non-occupational events. These unofficial, non-occupational events may include "supposedly informal" dinner gatherings after work, which often involve alcohol consumption. While dinner gatherings are becoming less and less common with the rise of an individualistic culture among the younger generation today, the older generation expects juniors to join them for dinner. However, some juniors may still want to join because their *chemyeon* tells them seniors will favor those who have dinner and drink together. This is not just for getting know each other, but mostly for talking shop which fosters a sense of family, *uliseong*. This strengthens organizational communication, which, in turn, will result in organizational performance.

Dark side of chemyeon

Despite its positive contributions to the Korean bureaucracy culture, *chemyeon* sometimes causes problems. When higher officials are interrogated by prosecutors, they fear to be known as felons. Some of them even commit suicide before they are found guilty of crimes. A hypocritic *chemyeon* is more valued than a person's life. To those who really mind what other would think about theme may have made such choice to claim they are clean, but giving up life to save one's *chemyeon* may be inappropriate for justice. In other words, *Cheymoyon* makes public officials ethical before the temptation of corruption, because, for example, they will calculate the social cost of corruption which is losing *chemyeon*, not just punishment in the case of an investigation. *Uliseong* putting emphasis on an organizational level instead of individual level also increases ethical behavior in this regard. If one of the organizational members is discovered to be involved in a scandal, the organizational members will not consider it just as an individual level of deviation, but as a shame of their organization, i.e. losing the organization's *chemyeon*.

In short, *chemyeon* and *uliseong* are the two psychological features that build up a unique aspect of competition within Korean bureaucracy. While *chemyeon* mitigates the side effects of intra-organizational competition by minimizing embarrassment from defeat, *uliseong* controls excessive intra-organizational competition and bolsters interorganizational competition. These two concepts are key mechanisms of competition, which are the foundations of a competitive organization.

Moving forward, this section can be closed by acknowledging that Korean bureaucrats tend to have a strong sense of organizational identification (Im & Park, 2015), and sometimes appear in a form of *uliseong*, influencing the competitive state. Identifying oneself with his or her branch functions as a motivation for competition, and reduces bureaucratic inertia. And because the resulting inter-organizational competition has had a positive effect on members' performance and the overall organizational outcome, competition should be recognized as a core performance characteristic of the Korean bureaucracy.

Closing remarks

Chapter 2 explains how individual behavior toward competition played an important role in economic development in South Korea. After the Korean War, in the absence of a traditional social class system, there were relatively equal opportunities for anyone to move upward socially and economically. A strong desire of people to escape poverty affected economic growth, which led to a fierce competition for entering the newly created social classes: a middle class and an educated class. People oriented to competition were motivated to work hard as the government also created a competitive environment for national development. At the same time, *uliseong* and *chemyeon* worked as a buffer against excessive competition.

Notes

1 Fatalism is generally defined as "the belief that good or ill fortune, and every form of blessing or disaster is determined by supernatural forces beyond the reach of human power" (Paik, 1978: 202).
2 Familism is defined as "a form of social organization in which all values are determined by reference to the maintenance, continuity, and functions of the family group" (Kulp, 1925).
3 In general, average years for promoting chief official (Class 5) to secretary official (Class 4) is 11 years in MOSF and nine years for other departments (http://www.ebn.co.kr/news/view/800145/ZM1).
4 *Gwanpia* is a compound word for *Gwanryo* (bureaucrat in Korean) and Mafia.

References

Bista, D. B. (1991). *Fatalism and Development: Nepal's Struggle for Modernization*. Calcutta, India: Orient Blackswan.
Brighouse, H., & Swift, A. (2006). Equality, priority, and positional goods. *Ethics*, 116(3), 471–497.

Choi, S. J., Jung, Y. J., & Im, T. B. (2018). Effects of trait competitiveness on ethical attitudes in the public sector: The moderation effect of a performance-oriented climate. *Korean Public Administration Review*, 52(3), 291–317.

Festinger L. (1954). A theory of social comparison processes. *Human Relations*, 7, 117–140.

Furnham, A., Kirkcaldy, B. D., & Lynn, R. (1994). National attitudes to competitiveness, money, and work among young people: First, second, and third world differences. *Human Relations*, 47(1), 119–132.

Garcia, S. M., Song, H., & Tesser, A. (2010). Tainted recommendations: The social comparison bias. *Organizational Behavior and Human Decision Processes*, 113(2), 97–101.

Graziano, W. G., & Eisenberg, N. (1997). Agreeableness: A dimension of personality. In Hogan, R., Johnson, J., & Briggs, S. (Eds.). *Handbook of Personality Psychology*. San Diego, CA: Academic, pp. 795–824.

Griffin-Pierson, S. (1990). The competitiveness questionnaire: A measure of two components of competitiveness. *Measurement & Evaluation in Counseling & Development*, 23(3), 108–115.

Hofstede, G. (2011). Dimensionalizing cultures: The Hofstede model in context. *Online Readings in Psychology and Culture*, 2(1), 1–26.

Im, T. (2018). *Public Administration: From the Perspective of Time*. Seoul: Park Young-sa.

Im, T., & Park, J. (2015). Interorganizational competition and government competitiveness: The case of the Korean Central Government. *The Korean Journal of Policy Studies*, 30(2), 93–118.

Kang, M. (2011). The impact of the Korean War on the political-economic system of South Korea: Economic growth and democracy. *International Journal of Korean Studies*, 15(1), 129–153.

Kim, D. (1990). The transformation of familism in modern Korean society: From cooperation to competition. *International Sociology*, 5(4), 409–425.

Koo, H. (2018). Rethink the middle class in Korea. *The Quarterly Changbi*, 40(1), 403–421.

Kulp, D. H. (1925). *Country Life in South China: The Sociology of Familism*, Vol. 1. New York city: Bureau of Publications, Teachers College, Columbia University.

Lee, H. B. (1966). Articles; from ecology to time – Time orientation approach to development administration (in Korean). *Korean Journal of Public Administration*, 4(2), 2001–2020.

Lee, H. B. (1982). *Future, Innovation, and Development*. Seoul: Panmun Book Company.

Lee, S., & Brinton, M. C. (1996). Elite education and social capital: The case of South Korea. *Sociology of Education*, 69, 177–192.

Mudrack, P. E., Bloodgood, J. M., & Turnley, W. H. (2012). Some ethical implications of individual competitiveness. *Journal of Business Ethics*, 108, 347–359.

Newby, J. L., & Klein, R. G. (2014). Competitiveness reconceptualized: Psychometric development of the competitiveness orientation measure as a unified measure of trait competitiveness. *The Psychological Record*, 64(4), 879–895.

Nisbett, R. (2004). *The Geography of Thought: How Asians and Westerners Think Differently... and Why*. New York: Simon and Schuster.

Oh, H. (2017). The effects of face-saving and group orientation of public organization members on organizational commitment: A focus on the mediating effect of person-organization fit. *Journal of Competency Development & Learning*, 12(4), 1–22.

Paik, W. (1978). Psycho-cultural approach to the study of Korean bureaucracy. In Kim, S. J., & Kang, C. W. (Eds.). *Korea: A Nation in Transition*. Seoul: Research Center for Peace and Unification.

Ryckman, R. M., Libby, C. R., van den Borne, B., Gold, J. A., & Lindner, M. A. (1997). Values of hypercompetitive and personal development competitive individuals. *Journal of Personality Assessment*, 69(2), 271–283.

Smith, R. H., Merlone, U., & Duffy, M. K. (2016). *Envy at Work and in Organizations*. New York: Oxford University Press.

Sorensen, C. W. (1994). Success and education in South Korea. *Comparative Education Review*, 38(1), 10–35.

Van de Vliert, E., Kluwer, E. S., & Lynn, R. (2000). Citizens of warmer countries are more competitive and poorer: Culture or chance? *Journal of Economic Psychology*, 21(2), 143–165.

Yang, I. (2016). A Study on the Influence of Psychological Competitiveness in Public Enterprises over Intrinsic Job Motivation (unpublished master's thesis). Seoul National University, Seoul.

3 Competition within an organization

This chapter extends the concept of *competitiveness* to all levels by first reviewing different forms of organization – family, school, workplace, and even public organizations – to understand the dominant competition-oriented culture in Korean society. It then identifies the family as the preliminary stage of competition among individuals, because the competition to earn more or at least equal portion of limited family resources leads to concentration of resources in the best-performing child. While a similar pattern is evident in other forms of organizations, and although the best-performing members are expected to help enhance the performance of affiliated organizations, a desire for a better position within the group drives individuals to compete with others. The chapter also points out the potential connection between competition and the collectivist nature inherent in Korean society.

Competition with whom?

The previous chapter on competing for oneself does not limit our discussion to psychological analysis. Becoming a better person naturally requires a standard to compare oneself against before putting in efforts to after results. Only with a standard will a person be able to properly measure his or her own accomplishments. This attains to an absolute level and a relative level of achievements. For example, an increase from 70 points to 90 points out of 100 points on an exam shows a 20-point achievement in absolute values. But what if the rank was important? The absolute point increase may fail to demonstrate a true increase in one's accomplishment. His or her rank may have become higher or lower, depending on how well others did on the same exam.

Competing with others thus becomes irresistible. Festinger (1950, 1954) has proposed a social comparison theory in which a person evaluates himself based on how his capabilities, opinions, and behaviors compare with "others". Once a person is able to observe how well others perform, one will have to look for the reason for not having done better, or at least as well as others. The exam that classifies ranks is a simple example of competition. However, competition with others is more inherent and natural than one might think. Competition exists in every form of organization: family, friends, colleagues, and countries.

A family driven society

Competitiveness is an inherent feature of Korean society. Why do Koreans compete so fiercely? We might find an answer from family and its functions, particularly during the developing era. Korea is well-known for its collectivist culture, and in a collective culture, individuals are more tied down for the sake of the groups' interests (Hofstede, 2011). A family is the most natural and ascribed group (or organization) that is given to a baby. Competition within a family was not just a matter of yearning to win over others, but a matter of survival during Korea's "compressed modernization" (Chang, 2010). Without guaranteed social security in the developing era, a family was the most reliable shelter for protecting one's material needs and physical safety let alone psychological comfort, and it was best if family members worked for the family's interests.

The collectivist nature of family was often shown when family served as a person's identity. The community identified people by their respective families. In traditional Korean society, sons and daughters were often recognized by their family name, Kim, Lee, and Park, to name a few. It was even difficult for neighbors to remember each child's name. Most households had extended families, with grandparents, parents, and many children living together. This was a common situation especially in rural areas because each person became part of the labor force that supports the family. With agriculture as the main industry until the 1960s, more children were an asset. More children meant more income. Family, especially a large family, provided resources for adapting to the rapidly changing society. Because a larger family enabled each family member to concentrate on obtaining different resources and share what others have brought, it was important for the family leader to determine what each person can best contribute. The ultimate goal of a family was to mobilize these contributions for the family's interests (Burgess & Locke, 1945) (Table 3.1).

Table 3.1 Korean households by type and average size

	One genera-tion	Two genera-tions	Three genera-tions	More than four generations	Single house-hold	Households w/unrelated persons	Average size of household
1955	–	–	–	–	3.2	–	–
1966	7.5	64.0	25.9	1.6	–	–	5.5
1970	6.8	70.0	22.1	1.1	0.0	0.0	5.2
1975	7.0	71.9	20.1	1.0	4.2	0.0	5.0
1980	9.0	74.2	17.8	0.6	4.8	1.5	4.5
1985	10.5	73.3	15.8	0.5	6.9	1.7	4.1
1990	12.0	74.1	13.6	0.3	9.0	1.5	3.7
1995	14.7	73.7	11.4	0.2	12.7	1.4	3.3

Source: Korean National Statistical Office. Annual Report on Vital Statistics (1982–1997).

Family bonding was essentially the single viable form of social capital during the transition from a rural agricultural society to an urban industrial society. Korean government in the developing era was incapable of providing proper social security to most of its people. Families had to financially support their members because an individual member could not afford enough time and opportunity due to a weak social safety net until the transition period to a welfare State in 1990s. Despite the apparent equality in mutual aid among its members, a micro-level view will show that family was run based on competition. Since each member was endowed with different abilities and capabilities, some were offered more resources than others. This often led to competition among children.

The Korean "instrumental familism" turned a family into the basic unit of competition in society. Competition among families was the vent of obsession for inter-generational class mobility. Once having confronted structural ceilings of inter-generational class mobility, many Korean parents expected their children to advance to a higher class on behalf of their families. Higher education, one of the principal means of enhancing social status, was at the center of solidifying families and mobilizing community resources. Brothers and sisters, not to mention parents, unsparingly sacrificed (under the name of 'investment') their time and opportunities to educate the eldest, (in most cases) firstborn son of the family. Successfully getting an admission to a prestigious college meant an increased possibility of a more successful life compared to others. A decent college degree almost guaranteed access to a decent job. If there were many siblings who wished to go to college, they needed to compete with each other for limited resource from their parents, because no other means such as student loans existed.

Competition at home: large family, fewer resources

In this sense, the Korean society during the rapid modernization era resembles that of family-oriented economies based on Max Weber's Protestantism (Chang, 2002: 143). Winning the competition for inter-generational class mobility is the dream of many families. Family members gladly support a young man's ambition. Therefore, education competition was not only about the individual itself but also about the familial desire for class mobility. Within-family competition was tense when Korean baby-boomers grew up. With limited resources but with a lot of siblings, a baby-boomer born during the post-Korean War period had to compete for their survival throughout their lives.

In recent years, inter-generational social mobility through higher education and parental sacrifice is getting harder and harder. According to the General Social Survey conducted by Statistics Korea, people are unlikely to believe that they can socially move upward, even if they work hard. Figure 3.1 shows that this pessimistic perspective on social mobility gets worse.

Despite limited family resources, many young Koreans made the most out of their endowments. Although they had to share a room, food, and clothes with their siblings, competitive people stood out among their families and peers. Sometimes competition between

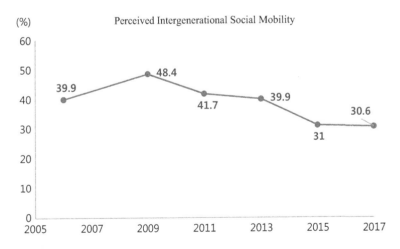

Figure 3.1 Changes in perceptions of inter-generational social class mobility in Korea.

Sources: Statistics Korea. General Social Survey (updated December 27, 2017) http://www.index.go.kr/potal/enaraIdx/idxField/userPageCh.do?idx_cd=4068.

siblings even made them achieve their goals together. A 1980 successful case involves Choi Yoon-hee, a 1982 New Delhi Asian Games medalist in swimming.[1] Her sister was a professional swimmer too, putting these sisters into a direct competition. The Choi sisters played in the same game, in which the elder sister Choi Yoon-jung checked a Japanese competitor, helping Yoon-hee defeat the competitor. In an interview, Choi Yoon-hee claimed that she had always been inferior to her elder sister while being the top among her peers. She also claimed that she started swimming because she was jealous of her sister winning a medal in a swimming competition. Although siblings from these two examples may or may not have experienced inadequate family resources, they have demonstrated the possibility of competition involving mutual assistance.

Parents' selective attention and financial support to children tend to bring siblings to a competition. Hierarchy issues often occur, as elders (especially eldest son) usually get the most support from parents. Siblings may not feel okay with this situation, and they may fight to gain at least equal resources with elders. When siblings compete for more resources and the competition turns out to be a success, at least one of them is able to provide for the entire family. Aside from internal achievements of providing for a family, a successful competition strengthens solidarity among the family. For example, once a son of a family gets into a top university, parents in the neighborhood start envying the family. In other cases, a family that has three PhDs in a row or university professors and judges are admired by other families as an academically well-achieved family. The environment around the family envies this successful family.

Competition at school

Koreans in general are sensitive to all kind of ranking as ranking used to be the 'one-and-only' criteria to judge students for teacher and children for parents. The 'ranking system' is blamed as an inhuman methodology to consider people as a product, but at the same time, it is the most fair system to distribute scarce resources.

The ranking system in class

Confucianism has long stressed the importance of respecting scholars in East Asia. Confucian culture has stimulated competition for better education, and most Koreans tend to look up to the prestigious top-tier schools and universities. The most elite path for the renowned education before the July 30th education system reform in 1980 was that of Gyeonggi (Boys) High School and Seoul National University. Alumnae from these schools have acquired most leadership positions throughout Korean communities. Prospective parents and students thus dreamed of admission from these schools as a guarantee to the highest positions in the social hierarchy. Parents in rural towns wanted to be just rich enough to afford their sons' top-class education in Seoul.

Parents, especially mothers who were housewives, were extremely competition-prone by all means to help their children get into decent universities. Faced with rising dissatisfaction from parents of unsuccessful children, the government's challenging mission was to set regulations to make them feel equally treated. The military government on July 30, 1980 had introduced a radical reform to ease the fierce competition for admission to prestigious colleges. It consisted of numerous education policies, but the two most significant were (1) setting an upper limit to the number of undergraduate degrees, and (2) abolishing respective universities' entrance exams. The second aimed at removing subjective evaluation tools that had been used to determine which students were most qualified to perform well in college entrance exams. Evaluation methods for students' performance had to be non-arguable, i.e. objective: a multiple-choice exam was the easy means of evaluating performance. By adopting this method, the Korean education system made *number competition* an essential mechanism of evaluation. Admission based on number competition has been widespread; all middle schools and high schools used to admit students on their numerical scores.

In Korea, unlike college admission in many other countries that manage to closely examine candidates' scholastic aptitudes and prospects in college education based on various perspectives not limited to exam scores, multiple-choice exam scores were the primary criteria for deciding whether a candidate was qualified. The national scholastic aptitude test (also known as Su-neung in Korean) that is organized just once a year by the Ministry of Education has long been accepted as an objective tool to line up students according to their scores.

Given this way of being placed by numeric order, students often felt extremely stressed by the competition. Students were not even permitted by their advisers to apply for certain colleges if they did not seem to be the top tier among applicants. Parents were ready to sacrifice themselves by doing anything that could help to improve their children's exam scores: paying for expensive cram schools or hiring private tutors. At this point, an old friend of childhood can simply turn into a competitor in high school. Then what happens to students for the rest of their lives is to compete with each other to get a higher grade point average (GPA) or rank higher than others. Life turns into a tough race to the extent that there is no room for a pure friendship.

Competing with friends and peers seems to have instigated social stress. Seventeen teenagers committed suicide in May and early June in 1988 for not having satisfactory school grades; one student wrote a letter that there was too much competition to bear.[2] The student feared school and exams, and this led to a miserable and unstable school life. In 1989, a high school student confessed to her mother that he would not be able to get into college; after his mother intoxicated herself and died, he did the same thing.[3] Competition among students became so fierce that many friendships were affected. In 1980, the government decided to increase the portion of GPA on college admission. Because the competition for better grades became more common, students started to not share their class notes with their friends.[4]

The July 30th education reform in 1980 increased the number of admissions by 30% for each university while keeping the number of undergraduate degrees per year. This meant that the additional 30% admitted would fail in the undergraduate program (Education Reform Commission, 1998). This policy had again generated incredible competition for grades among college students, and professors had to arrange a fair way to grade their exams. Many professors had to abandon their essay-style (and 'free-response') exams that were designed to measure students' logical thinking capacity. Instead, they adopted multiple-choice questions on most exams. Multiple-choice questions that have been widely used in primary and secondary schools were preferred to avoid any arguments from students having low grades. Students suffering from low GPA chose to exit from this competitive atmosphere by transferring to universities overseas, or by going to the army for three years. Consequently, the government considered the policy only a partial success and returned to the previous system that controlled the number of admitted students after seven years of experimentation in 1987.

College diploma as primary social identity

However, the strong competition explained above is just one side of a coin. Once students get high school diplomas and college degrees, their relationships enter a new stage. Once a competitor in life, a friend now becomes a person that may be helpful in making connections with others. When alumni work as higher officials in the government or executives in a sizable lucrative business, their friends tend to get more involvements than non-alumni. Even though friends work in different sectors and different industries, they may help each other. Now alumnae from different schools compete to increase their power within the social structure. This is when the collectivist nature within a group intensifies, and competition within a group turns into a competition with other groups.

These elite groups thus formed a sort of camaraderie, i.e. "esprit de corps", which was named *Uliseong* earlier. Public officials that had graduated from the prestigious schools have held major top positions in Korean government ministries and courts. People often call them influential elite bureaucrats, and they pursue their careers based on an extensive amount of social capital. These elite bureaucrats often accumulated social capital by developing close connections even with their elite alumnae in the private sector. The same social phenomenon continues even today with different high schools such as Daewon Foreign Language High School-Seoul National University graduates. These connections often involve favoritism and informal arrangements, which people often severely criticize for inequalities.

Competition at workplace: the private sector

Competition at a workplace is similar to competition at school. Competition is also embedded in many private sector human relationships. Whoever is employed with a handful of other employees happens to try really hard to stand out at his work. Because most companies in the private sector aim at maximizing profit, they want to produce and sell as much as possible at less cost. Performance evaluation for promotion and pay raise in the private sector is easier than in the public sector. Even if the Korean public sector has been stricter with a rank and seniority system for its employees, the deeper dimension of human relations in private companies remains the same to some extent.

Competition for better performance

Managing performance by putting cohorts in a competitive race is a common practice in the private sector, especially in the West. However, in Korea, private companies have a long tradition of collectivist culture, as William Ouchi & Price (1993) theorized for understanding Japanese companies planted in the United States. One can easily find the psychological characteristics, *Uliseong* and *Chemyeon* in the private companies as well.

POSCO, or Pohang Steel Corporation, was one of the first companies to adopt an incentive structure to promote competitive and efficient working environment[5] while still keeping a bureaucratic structure. While the company had been a State-owned company until its privatization in 2000, the founding CEO Park Tae-Jun in the earlier days attempted to find ways to encourage their employees to work harder by making the most out of the collective spirit. In addition to Western style performance evaluations introduced at the individual level, the company administration also awarded well-performing teams and departments. Also, most employees were paid according to their individual performance on top of a more traditional rank-basis compensation structure. Employees admit these managerial technics without reluctance thanks to its organization culture. Corporate culture was patriotic, and its core management philosophy was "Make Steel, Serve the Country" because the company was established with major funding from the settlement money for comfort women during the Japanese colonial period (Yoo, 2001: 34).

Many competitions at work helped companies achieve their performance goal, and sometimes even exceeded the goal. While positive aspects of competition have prevailed in many corporate success stories, news articles also have depicted negative effects of competition among employees. Too much competition among salesmen at a supermarket resulted in numerous fights, inappropriate marketing strategies, and excessive sales activities toward customers.[6] Competition often occurred for a better supermarket aisle that maximized the product exposure to customers. Salesmen's fights disturbed many customers' shopping experience. This competition at work even resulted in psychological adversity for many workers. Some even blamed for their colleagues for getting in competition.[7]

Private sector competition at work: "Samsung man" vs "LG man"

Despite some micro-level adversities, competition within private companies led to nation-wide competitions in different industries. For example, Samsung Electronics and LG Electronics (formerly Goldstar Electronics) have been competing in the Korean consumer electronics market since the 1980s. Employees at each company were eager to win a competition with their colleagues, and they were devoted to developing better breakthroughs than their competitors.

Once the best ideas from each company were produced and delivered to customers, the competition moved on to the next level: a battle between Samsung and LG. Consumers try to purchase the best product within their price range, so the only way to win in this battle was to mobilize a company's best resources for making an attractive product. Competitors in a company now united as "Samsung men" or "LG men" to perform better as a team. Employees of each company assimilate a collective culture of its own with a strong solidarity and strive to win the competition against its rivals. The competitive trait in this sense is fierce.

Competitions among Korean private companies were distinct from most other Western countries. In theory, the primary motivation in the private sector is profit maximization. However, most of Korean companies have acquired a special mind-set throughout the State-led developmental era. It can be characterized as a patriotic culture.

Back in 1945, only small and medium sized companies, mostly family businesses, existed. The growth of big conglomerates such as Samsung and LG, for example, went along with the economic miracle of the country. It was thanks to the government's developmental policies that these companies lacking in capital, technology, and experiences could grow. They were devoted to contributing to national projects. For example, Hyundai Company without having experience of big construction project was in charge of the national construction project of the first highway Seoul-Busan in 1970. Part of the reason for the contribution might be potential rewards such as future tax abatement and contracts, but the main reason was that many private businesses initially operated on government subsidies and public projects, which made them psychologically and economically dependent on the government.

Let alone State-owned, privatized companies maintain a somewhat patriotic culture which triggers a unique culture of competition vis-à-vis other countries. The teamwork of different companies throughout industries expedited the industrialization of Korea. Employees were highly motivated by the fact that they are important actors of the national economic development project. Therefore, unlike what is happening in other countries, the company's culture is still more collectivist when an issue relates to the national level. At the macro-level, competing individuals and companies united in their national identities, achieving the important national goal of economic growth.

Competition in the workplace: the public sector

Officialdom has long been dreamt of by many Korean young men. Most public positions in Korea have required passing national exams since at least the 9th century. National exams for public officials (or Civil Service Exams) have existed since the Shilla Dynasty before the 10th century. The Chosun Dynasty since the 13th century, until Japanese colonization, consisted of different classes. Mobility between classes was limited, but national exams for public officials gave equal opportunities to those who belonged to the literary class for competing and working in the government.[8] Those who passed the exam were given a job in the government; the entire process of public official recruitment was considered fair, as the exam tested intelligence instead of looking at one's background such as the noble of one's family.

In the Chosun Dynasty, the merit-based human resource system did not allow top officials, even kings, to hire those who did not pass the exams. According to Cha (2018), the national public official exam in the Chosun Dynasty pursued a pure meritocracy that made candidates compete. In addition to recruitment, a special exam reserved to incumbent officials, called *jungsi*, worked as an incentive in officials' promotion (Kim, 1998; Cha, 2018). Thus, a fair competition has long been institutionalized in the recruitment of public officials. Despite positive aspects of national exams and the initial intention to prevent the spoils system, some public official recruitments of lower ranks had been conducted based on favoritism (Lee, 2008). However, it is noticeable that merit recruitment prevailed largely throughout history. The Nonmerit system concerned only a small portion of the recruitees and was a side effect of the fierce competition for public officer positions among different power groups.

Even after the establishment of the Republic of Korea in 1948, being part of the government continued to be an honor to most families. Jobs in the public sector, schoolteachers, for example, were a rare category of jobs receiving a regular salary, especially in the rural area. The country was completely ruined after liberation from the Japanese colonial period and the Korean War; no big enterprises or industries existed. The central government was the only actor that could mobilize the limited resources, mainly foreign aid, to plan large projects within the country. On the other hand, private companies were underdeveloped: they lacked capital, technology, and talented human resources to start big projects.

Among talented young people hoping to be government employees, there has been always high competition for the entry into the government. Especially, in the development era, one of the main differences between public positions and private positions was whether applicants must take a national exam. Government positions were open for those who pass the national Civil Service Exam, which involves a highly rigorous and selective process. In order to pass the exam, one must win in the fierce competition with numerous young and competitive college graduates. After or during his prestigious college education, a bright young man usually spent another year for the preparation of national Civil Service Exams, which usually takes up to three to five years. Major private enterprises have adopted a similar selection procedure to the Civil Service Exam over the last two decades. As the private sector has become highly competitive and lucrative, more and more people wanted to be part of it. Competition for private positions is at least as high as that for public positions.

Why do Korean public employees keep competing? The rank system and the national exam make them compete in the first place. Civil service was not just a job among others, but was, de facto, considered as a social class. Job security with lifetime employment which is well theorized by W. Ouchi (Theory Z, 1993) as well as prestige and power which can be exercised in government regulation and resource allocation embedded this category of social class in Korean society.

However, higher rank and position alone do not mean anything. What makes people want a promotion to a higher position may be personal interests that become approachable in that position. Park (2013)'s research reveals that Korean bureaucrats' public service motivation (PSM) is based on personal interests and their power taste in the community. Aside from more general assumptions of the PSM model that focus on the self-sacrifice and compassion of public officials, Park suggests that competition for higher government positions has led to opportunistic behavior of public employees. Opportunistic behaviors often involve favoring family's business for government contracts or employing a relative for temporary positions. These behaviors do not directly benefit those in government positions but instead benefit people around them. This again is related to collectivism-led competitions. People get in numerous competitions to provide for and take care of their close friends and relatives, hoping to get their help in the future.

Rule of law: gap between rules and reality

Rule of law refers to a principle by which everyone is subject to comply with written codes without exception. Ruling the people by laws in the strict sense of the term did not exist in traditional Korean society. For example, the Chosun Dynasty, a precedent of the Republic of Korea, was based on the self-regulating nature of individual communities. A self-regulation was built on a set of morale for the rulers, leaving rule of law as unnecessary in the Chosun society. An ethical society that Confucius dreamed of did not require laws. The ruling elite including the kings should be an ethical exemplar to the people, while the people were supposed to follow these moral leaders. If detailed and written codes as laws existed, it was a leader's virtue to bend 'rules' in a broad sense of the term, such as precedents of similar cases to benefit the people.

Korea has adopted rule of law from Western countries. Modernization in the Korean public sphere meant the introduction of the Western style rule of law. In the developmental era, one of the main tasks of the high officials was to write rules and prepare texts of law proposals to the parliament, mainly by replicating Western examples. Therefore, the social norm widespread in the modern Korean society conflicted with the laws introduced without deeply considering their applicability.

For example, in the transition era, most ordinary citizens were not used to queue before ticket offices such as railway stations or bus terminals. In those days, it was common to observe some people cutting in line everywhere. People criticized this problem by pointing out the lack of citizenship. But easier said than done. In order to truly understand the problem, one should take consideration into the highly competitive condition due to supply constraints. For them, pushing in line, often without asking excuse to those lining behind, does not mean simply whether to appear to be nice to others, but to miss or not the train they wanted to travel with. Therefore law reinforcement or compliance was difficult.

Facing a huge gap between what laws prescribe and the reality, many Korean communities expected flexibility in laws, thus considering it okay to break laws. It has become common sense to consider law enforcement as impotent, especially toward higher public officials and the privileged (Im, 2007: 11). Thus, people were prone to abide by rules and laws only to their benefits, and they said it is okay to break them if they can win in a competition. People asked for laws to protect their rights, inconsiderate of others' rights. Egalitarianism, or wishing for an equal treatment with others, can be an explanatory factor of such a phenomenon. Superiority, or trying to become better than others, can be another. Despite the lasting widespread notion that it is okay to break the law for one's benefits, 64% of Koreans that have responded to the 2017 Korea Social Integration Survey think that law execution in Korea is mostly unfair, and 86% of the same sample think administration procedures should be more transparent than they are now (Korea Institute of Public Administration, 2017). These recent survey results convey a mature citizenship now becoming more and more prevalent in Korean society, but this was not the case in the developmental era. In the 1960s–1970s, the Korean government had initiated a public campaign (movement) to promote citizens' lining up. Cutting-in-line was quite universal in Korean society, making public spaces and public services chaotic. On the other hand, speeding on a highway became another problem, mainly due to lack of speed cameras and proper speeding ticket issuances. Most people were selfish to think only about their own benefits. These measures were the first and easier actions to bring rule of law into life in Korean communities.

From these simple experiences, we may now notice that the Western legal structure does not always apply to the Korean, or Asian, context. Korean people, with the insufficient gross amount of resources, quite naturally leaned toward reckless behaviors. Competition was simply ubiquitous: getting on a bus during rush hours to and from work, racing for decently priced goods and services, and going to a prestigious college. Every minute in a day was spent competing with other people. A slight deviation from rules nearly guaranteed quite a fortune. Being unofficially aware of local developments prior to official announcement brought an extensive amount of profits to an exclusive group of people. Knowing about changes to college admission policies before anyone else guaranteed immediate superiority over other candidates.

Aside from people's lack of attention to the rule of law, the extreme information asymmetry of the Korean legal structure also added to legal ignorance. Unlike in the 2000s when Internet access has started to become a universal source of information, most Korean people had to suffer through a lack of information. These limited amounts of information were often found to be late and erroneous, keeping people confused about what is okay to do and what is not. For those who inappropriately bypassed laws or deliberately broke them, all they had to do was to pretend not to have broken the law, or even pretend to be unaware of it. These people were only concerned about their benefits and goal accomplishments; they did not care if they abided by rules or not. Those who happened to follow the rules almost felt they were losing in the law game. However, this lack of attention to the law has decreased in recent decades, making it a social norm for most citizens to follow their communities' rules.

Concluding remarks

Chapter 3 mainly discusses different stages of a competition and underlying cultures in Korea. First, discussion on *competitiveness* at the individual level from Chapter 2 is developed in this chapter, with an introduction of social comparison theory as a major framework of intra-organizational competitions. This chapter also suggests family as the preliminary stage of an intra-organizational competition, establishing the cultural background for competition at school and work. Anecdotal cases further clarify the phenomena of resource concentration in the best-performing child of the family. A similar discussion with different levels of organizations, such as schools, private companies, and public organizations, has come to the conclusion that the best-performing members are expected to help enhance the overall performance of their organizations, and desire for a better position within an organization keeps people competing with others. Lastly, the potential connection between competition and collectivist nature in the Korean society is proposed through concrete examples. The chapter is a bridge between Chapter 2, which talks about theoretical and psychological backgrounds of individual competitiveness at the micro-level, and Chapter 4, which begins to examine inter-organizational competitiveness at the macro-level.

Notes

1 The Dong-A Ilbo. The Dong-A Ilbo Person of the year "Choi Yoon-hee". December 30, 1982.
2 The Kyunghyang Shinmun. "Teen suicide and the trap of education". June 11, 1988.
3 The Dong-A Ilbo. "No confidence to pass the college admission", Mother and son committed suicide by taking poison. December 26, 1989.
4 The Kyunghyang Shinmun. High school "Yalgae" losing their friendship. November 11, 1983.
5 Maeil Business Newspaper. Contribute to the improvement of performance. August 20, 1974.
6 Maeil Business Newspaper. The excessive competition of the sales promotion personnel dispatched form Supermarket, Consumer felt "displeasure". September 12, 1983.
7 The Kyunghyang Shinmun. Mental health, Korean reflected by the "ui-chang". It is impossible to always get ahead of other. January 22, 1985.
8 Men from the lowest class such as butchery were not allowed to apply to these exams.

References

Burgess, E. W., & Locke, H. J. (1945). *The Family: From Institution to Companionship*. Oxford, England: American Book Co.
Cha, S. (2018). The Confucian meritocracy and personnel appointment during the Chosŏn Dynasty (Unpublished doctoral dissertation). Seoul National University, Seoul, South Korea.

Chang, K. (2002). *South Korea under Compressed Modernity: Familial Political Economy in Transition*. Abingdon and New York: Routledge Advances in Korean Studies.

Chang, K-S. (2010). *South Korea under Compressed Modernity: Familial Political Economy in Transition*. New York: Routledge.Education Reform Commission. (1998). *Development Index of Korean Education in the 21st Century*. Seoul: Education Reform Commission.

Festinger, L. (1950). Informal social communication. *Psychological Review*, 57(5), 271–282.

Festinger, L. (1954). A theory of social comparison processes. *Human Relations*, 7(2), 117–140.

Hofstede, G. (2011). Dimensionalizing cultures: The Hofstede model in context. *Online Readings in Psychology and Culture*, 2(1), 1–26.

Im, T. (2007). In search of a theoretical model for explaining the phenomena of Korean public administration. *Korean Governance (in Korean), Korean Governance Review*, 14(1), 1–30.

Kim, C. (1998). Study of early Joseon state examination system. *Treatises on Korean History*, 80, 91–130.

Korea Institute of Public Administration. (2017). *Korea Social Integration Survey*. Seoul: Korea Institute of Public Administration.

Lee, N. (2008). The state examination system, its lights, and shadows. *Issues in East-Asian Philosophy*, 18, 117–136.

Ouchi, W. G., & Price, R. L. (1993). Hierarchies, clans, and theory Z: A new perspective on organization development. *Organizational dynamics*, 21(4), 62–71.

Park, J. (2013). Exploratory Study on the Applicability of the Public Service Motivation Concept to South Korea. Doctoral dissertation. The University of Pittsburgh.

Statistics Korea. General Social Survey (updated 27 Dec 2017). http://www.index.go.kr/potal/enaraIdx/idxField/userPageCh.do?idx_cd=4068

Yoo, H. (2001). Policy change and policy entrepreneurs (in Korean). *Korean Journal of Public Administration*, 39(1), 23–42.

4 Competing with an organization

This chapter explains about the inter-organizational competition. In particular, this chapter sheds light on what is happening in the public organization body. Previous chapters have already described competition as a result of Korean society's unique organizational culture of familism and collectivism. Along this vein, the chapter discusses Korea's typical decision-making process, *Pumyui system*, which projects the collective mechanism inside the hierarchical bureaucracy. With regard to inter-organizational competition, the chapter mainly focuses onorganization to organization competition: among central government ministries and agencies, and executive-legislative relation in Korea.

Collectivity within the organization mechanism

Competition needs at least a minimum level of coordination to produce a certain efficiency. Intra-organizational competition implies "the coordination processes within a multiunit organization that within an organization requires formal hierarchical structure and informal lateral relations as coordination mechanisms" (Tsai, 2002).

Decision-making system: Pumyui

The Korean bureaucracy is especially notorious for its complicated and slow decision-making process, known as *Pumyui*, which is a deeply rooted trait along with the history of the government (Im, 2010). The word *Pumyui* originally means consulting with a superior prior to final approval (Cho & Im, 2016: 280). *Pumyui system* consists of two conceptual ideas: 'official document' and assuring 'consensus'.

'Official document' flow indicates a formal and visible navigation of official documents inside a bureaucracy. If one observes what is happening inside of a government building, one can easily spot this particular way of circulating a written document that requires approved signatures alongside the formal hierarchy. Such an act of establishing a document at the starting point is called *kian*, a draft. Although it is called a draft, contents should be accompanied with pieces of evidence if necessary, since this document will be reviewed and revised by superiors. Usually, *kian* is drafted by entry or junior level officials under the guidance of their manager (or supervisor). The supervisors, one by one, will read the draft and, if not satisfied, correct the contents and return it to the subordinates to revise them. If there is any other opinion to the draft, those can be indicated in the original document or a separate sheet.

In this way, the junior knocks doors of the superiors and gets additional tips, and this is the opportunity to have face-to-face contact with the bosses. For example, in the central administrative agency, the approval process starts from a junior level manager and ends at the minister. *Kian* usually circulates from a unit organization to top its executives, but it may also be transferred to other units (even other ministries) when the case needs to be reviewed by related units or requires notification and cooperation. Figures 4.1 and 4.2 illustrate how official documents are circulated in *Pumyui* process.

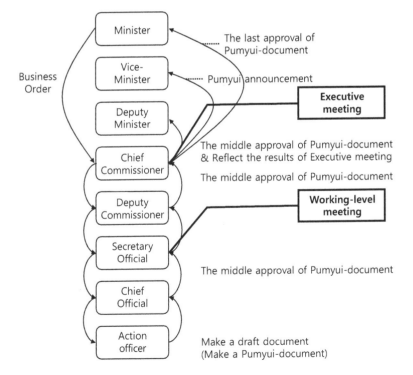

Figure 4.1 Pumyui procedures.

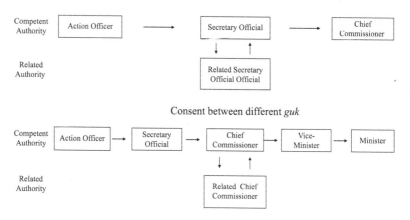

Figure 4.2 Pumyui procedures.
Source: Modified from Cho (1984: 116).

This way of sharing information assures consensus among organization members. The official document will not arrive at the top final decision maker until all concerned actors have approved it. Unlike in most Western bureaucracies often characterized by stalled hierarchy, *Pumyui* guarantees vertical communication (cf. Crozier, 1964). In addition, *Pumyui* imposes a unit of organization to obtain approval from concerned members of the same hierarchy. This contrasts with the Western style of a meeting where all members physically gather in the same place to discuss. As a matter of fact, there usually are numerous informal conversations and formal meetings involving diverse actors before the official document begins to move around. If neither informal nor formal interactions occur beforehand, the document can encounter unprecedented obstacles. In other words, this particular way of coordination and cooperation requires informal lateral relationships. Before expressing opinions on the document, concerned officials usually need face-to-face communication in advance.

Pumyui system allows the head of an agency to be aware of every issue being considered in the agency, without exception. Thus, it tends to be very time-consuming. Since the e-government reforms in the late 1990s in favor of 'paperless office', most of the paper documents have been replaced by electronic signing.

Consensus and authority

Pumyui system is often blamed as the redundant duplication process that causes inefficient mechanisms of decision-making in an organization. However, it is a characteristic of traditional cooperative decision-making processes that emphasize collectivism and loyalty. Collective and centralized decision-making systems reflect the familism administrative culture of Korea. In Korea's traditional parent to child relationship, the patriarchal culture was dominant in that a father owned all the authority, and children had to consult and confirm all matters with their parents – usually their fathers. This phenomenon also appears in administrative organizational culture. Furthermore, confirming and consulting with supervisors tend to provide the opportunity to contact and be recognized by them, and show loyalty and virtue at the same time.

This relates to the essence of Confucian culture which identifies all relationships between people as a hierarchy. Confucianism always defines a relationship as a vertical relationship, except for friendships. Hierarchical relationship applies to the ruler-ruled relationship, husband-wife relationship, parents-children relationship, brother-brother, and the teacher-student relationship. In that relationship, the former should have authority, and the latter should obey and fully respect the other. This type of obedience should be nuanced as a kind of accepted authority, in contrast to a forced submission which means a reluctant submission to an authority they do not accept. This difference can be understood if one recalls Philip Selznick's definition of "authority", which falls into the zone of acceptance of subordinates (Selznick, 1948). Thus, the critical condition for the Korean model of the decision process is that a ruler is supposed to be an ethical role model to the ruled. The Confucian culture is inherited by the authoritarian culture in the Korean bureaucracy.

Collectivism embedded in formal organization structures

Ministries and agencies

The structure of the Korean Central Government is designed in a hierarchical way. There is a clear chain of command starting from the president to heads of Administration through prime minister and minister in charge. The principle relates to the classical principle of scientific management: separation of line organizations as opposed to the staff organizations (Im, 2016). The administrative management school thinks that the most important administrative ideology of government organizations is efficiency. Division of tasks and specialization are considered crucial in achieving efficiency; coordinating and managing these tasks is another important job required for efficient organizations.

In this context, the Korean government enacted the 'Government Organization Act', which sets up the establishment, organization, and scope of the administrative agencies for the unified and systematic execution of the administrative affairs of the state. Since its inaction in 1948, the act has been revised 55 times to enable a more systematic and streamlined administration of government organizations. It particularly emphasizes regulation for and coordination of systematic organizations.

For example, the Blue House, which is directly under the supervision of the president, is divided into the 'Presidential Office' and the 'National Security Office'. In order to assist in the tasks of the secretary general, the policy director, and the national security officer of these direct organizations, the chief of staff, economic leader, and NSC secretary function as subordinates or sub-organizations. In this way, each government organization has a hierarchical relationship with its parent organizations and sub-organizations. This vertical relationship continuously adapts and changes to accommodate the efficient processing of tasks. In other words, the coordination mechanism of government organizations assures division of labor, making their sub-departments strive for overall efficiency.

Organizational design within a ministry

According to the Government Organization Act (2nd clause of the 2nd article), *Bu*, *Cheo*, and *Cheong* are designated as subunits of the central government organization. The central government is the executive branch and, as a presidential system, is headed by the president according to the Constitution. The prime minister assists the president and supervises administrative branches, each of which is mostly *Bu* organizations led by ministers. This section intends to give a brief introduction to the three key organizational units and their hierarchical relationships, which are designed for the coherence of various government activities (Figure 4.3).

Ministry (Bu, 部)

A *Bu* organization is the basic unit of the central government (Min, 2006). Other forms of organizations such as ministries (*Cheo*), agencies (*Cheong*), and commissions mainly supplement functions of *Bu*.

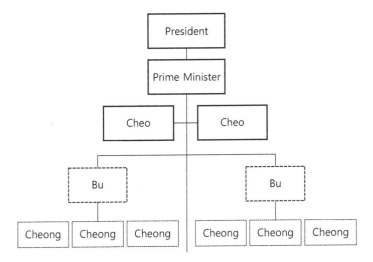

Figure 4.3 Organigram of the Korean central government.

Each *Bu* has its distinct mission under the supervision of the president and the prime minister. More specifically, *Bu* is stipulated by the Constitution, which says that "the president shall appoint, with recommendation from the prime minister, heads of executive ministries (*Bu*) among members of the state council" (Article 94), and

> the prime minister or the head of each executive ministry (*Bu*) may, under powers delegated by the Act or Presidential Decree, or ex officio, issue ordinances of the prime minister or the executive ministry concerning matters that are within their jurisdiction.
>
> (Article 95)

*Staff Ministry (*Cheo, 處*)*

As a central government organization under the command of the prime minister, *Cheo* organizations generally are staff organizations, covering overall tasks of the executive branch. Although the official English name is the same as Bu, a *Cheo* organization is supposed to support *Bu* and *Cheong*, operating as a staff organization of the executive branch rather than directly serving citizens. One of the core functions of a *Cheo* organization is to provide technical and procedural support; its organizational environment is stable, and the degree of formality and centrality is relatively high, whereas the level of complexity is low (Lee & Oh, 2014: 104).

*Agency (*Cheong, 廳*)*

The purpose of a *Cheong* organization is to share the workload of a *Bu* organization, i.e. tasks that are mostly policy implementation-oriented yet functionally independent (Kim, 2000). Outcomes of a *Cheong* organization are more tangible than those of other government organizations because it functions as an implementing organization backed up by routine tasks and specialties. Owing to its purpose of establishment, the evaluation of performance measures is relatively straightforward and most of the tasks involve direct contact with citizens providing administrative services. However, the scope of administration has rapidly increased in modern society and it has become realistically almost impossible for *Cheong* organizations to function only as implementing organizations.

Competition and bureaucratic expansion

From the standpoint of legal status, all ministries are endowed with equal authority and responsibility. For example, the same salary scale is applied to all ministers; vice-ministers and heads of administration are paid the same amount, which is of course less than what the minister is paid. Managerial costs for each agency are allocated on the basis of equality, calculated by certain criteria. Although there exists an ordering protocol for ministers to take the president's duty in case of his/her unexpected vacancy, ministers are equal in terms of their jurisdictional powers.

However, this equal treatment triggers a desire to be superior vis-à-vis others because many organizational members have strong appetites for power. The growth in size means more human resources, which will allow agencies to work more and prove their *raison d'être*. The Bureau of Organization that is normally attached to the Ministry of General Affairs has a power to maintain a small and efficient government. In contrast, most other ministries mobilize all means to expand their sizes. It has become all agency's dream to expand and become a *Bu*. This phenomenon can also be theoretically explained by Parkinson' law and Niskanen's theory of bureaucratic expansion.

Bureaucracies inherently tend to expand. Parkinson argued that the increase in the number of civil servants derives from the mind that the public servants want to increase their power by increasing the number of their subordinates, and it leads to an increase in the number of tasks. This process is repeated, and the bureaucracy always wants to expand. In Parkinson's law, bureaucrats are lazy and insensitive to efficiency.

Most Korean administrative organizations prefer to constantly expand, especially to '*Bu*' organizations. A *Bu* organization enjoys a superior legal status to *Cheong* and certain *Cheo* organizations because of its status as a member of the cabinet meeting, and at the same time, its right to directly submit the bill to the National Assembly. Along with the legislative power, *Bu* organizations have the right to plan, coordinate, and acquire implementing power. Implementing policies and programs is desirable because it is directly related to securing budgets, which is pivotal in increasing the size of the organization. In this sense, elevating the organizational status to a *Bu* level is the goal of power game among employees of *Cheo* and *Cheong* agencies. The power game finally achieves its goal when an organization gains its status as a core agency that may solve certain emerging social issues.

While the bureaucracy tries to expand its own resources and gain autonomy from the outside, its activities are often limited due to political and legal constraints. Many organizations try to overcome this problem by establishing an auxiliary agency that is less susceptible to restrictions. In other words, a public agency is a preferred way to expand organizations. Most public agencies help their parent organizations to avoid political criticism and accountability while still achieving their goals (e.g. organizational expansion). As a result, since only a limited number of agencies can become *Bu* organizations, numerous agencies struggle over just a few slots. Therefore, the Korean government system itself is a "competition model" (Im, 2014: 39) that consists of continuously competing subordinate organizations.

Table 4.1 shows how the number of government organizations changed – mostly in a positive direction – since the Korean government has been established. It is obvious that the number of *Bu* organizations has continuously increased. Other levels of organizations such as *Won* (院, board), *Cheo* (處, staff ministry), *Cheong* (廳, administration), and staff committees show ups and downs in their numbers. These observations support that sub-*Bu* organizations have encountered endless cycles of birth and death. While these numbers only appear to provide evidence for relatively stable growth of *Bu* organizations, these organizations have also experienced major changes and survivals.

Birth and death of organizations

Korean government organizations have confronted major structural changes over their 70 years of history. As mentioned throughout this chapter, major features of those changes pertain to bureaucratic expansion, instead of downsizing or abolishment. Although a number of

Table 4.1 Changes in Korean central government organizations

Amendment	President	Year	Total	Won	Bu	Cheo	Cheong	Etc.[a]
1st	Lee S.	1948	18	–	11	4	–	3
2nd		1954	18	–	12	2	3	1
3rd	Yoon B.	1960	20	1	12	1	3	33
4th		1961	23	2	13	3	2	3
5th	Park J.	1963	27	2	13	3	5	4
6th		1970	38	2	13	4	12	7
7th		1973	37	2	13	4	13	5
8th	Chun D.	1981	42	2	15	4	14	7
9th	Roh T.	1989	39	2	16	6	12	3
	Kim Y.	1993	39	2	14	6	15	2
	Kim D.	1998	36	–	17	2	16	1
	Roh M.	2004	39	–	18	4	17	–
	Lee M.	2013	35	–	15	2	18	–
	Park G.	2016	38	2	17	5	16	5
	Moon J.	2018	40	–	18	5	17	–

Source: Modified from Min (2006: 3).

a Etc.: External bureaus and committees.

organizations have been abolished, only a few were completely abolished. Most have been merged with other organizations – ministries, and even bureaus and departments – while maintaining their core functions. Many presidents have tried to restructure fundamentally the government structure. They have encountered various forms of resistances from administrative units operating on a strong solidarity, *Uliseong*. As a result, over last decades, the total number of newly established organizations was twice that of abolished agencies. Due to organizational competition, it turned out extremely difficult to abolish an agency. This is the reason why most of the reforms were concentrated on the attitudinal changes and the process, and the reform process of a structural change was secretive to avoid resistance (Im, 2011). In other words, the most critical reason such an important decision was made covertly was 'power dynamics' rather than logical debate. Power dynamics has been the strongest (if not the only) impetus for restructuring. Since restructuring is a matter of life and death for related organizations, concealing organizational strategy and political intentions from competitors was pivotal, making the whole process buttoned up.

This competition game tells that whatever happens inside the government system is all about power. The people within have witnessed throughout the time how powerful organizations wield absolute power and authority over relatively weaker organizations, ultimately leading to the "discordance between responsibilities and authorities" in many cases (Cho & Im, 2016). A typical example of such discordance is wielding power beyond what is specified in the positive law (e.g. the Ministry of Economy and Finance taking de facto control over many other ministries through budgetary authority). Authority in personnel management is another effective weapon to control and draw loyalty from individuals. Thus, the relationships of organizations and sub-departments, along with how they interact with surrounding environments, and interpersonal relationships can all be understood by power struggle.

Inter-organization competition: resource allocation

The cyclic character of budgeting, which consists of a successive process of budget proposals and decisions, generates a particular phenomenon in the Korean public sector strongly marked by competition. In the process of budgeting formation, i.e. next year's budget proposal to be submitted to the Congress, there often are pork barrel games to have a larger allotment of the budget among organizations in the executive branch. Each ministry manages to exaggerate its necessary budget and sometimes includes unnecessary expenditures. Instrumentalism is a realistic view to explain many government decisions on budget formation amid the growing economy in Korea.

Guardian and advocate

Wildavsky (1975) emphasized different roles played by a spending department and a treasury department during the budget-making process. He labeled spending departments "advocates" for expenditures; he called budgeting officials "guardians" of the public's purse. In this context, it is inevitable for the 'advocate' organization to request more funds than they are likely to receive, while 'guardians' will try to make sure that the budget does not exceed available resources.[1] The latter, therefore, have a prime role of trimming and cutting requests from numerous organizations (Rosenberg & Tomkins, 1983) (Table 4.2).

The competition for the larger budget can arise due to the information asymmetry between two actors, i.e. Ministry of Economy and Finance and each ministry and agency. Multiple advocates knowing ins and outs will provide only favorable information to support their budget proposals, leaving guardians with limited information to make decisions with. Guardians still need to follow the timeline according to the budget cycle, and they have no extra time to further investigate beyond given information. Each ministry and agency, or

Table 4.2 Major actors and their roles in the budget process

Stage Role	Budget preparation	Resolution stage for budget-bill deliberation		
		Entire process	Standing committee	Special committee on budget and accounts
Advocate	Ministries and agencies	Executive branch (MEF)	Ministries and agencies	Ministries and agencies
Guardian	Ministry of Economy and Finance (MEF)	Congress	A standing member	A member of the special committee on budget and accounts

Source: Reorganized from Im (2018: 339–355).

advocate, then wants to stand out by committing a moral hazard: to exaggerate the amount of budget demand. These budget requests should be based on annual experiences, but ministries and agencies are fully aware of the fact that their initial proposal will be cut due to limited government financial resources for the following fiscal year. Moreover, if ministries request just the right amount of budget based solely on previous experiences, it becomes more difficult to request more even when the government revenue is expected to grow the following year. In the resolution stage, the budget proposed by the Executive branches, which is represented by the Ministry of Economy and Finance, the Budget Bureau, more precisely, is reviewed and approved by the Congress. In this process, the advocate is the Executive branches and the guardian is the Congress. The Congress oversees the executive budget not to waste taxes collected from citizens. Standing committees of the Congress conduct a preliminary review of the budget and then notify the result to the Special committee on budget and accounts. Once the executive budget is in the process of being deliberated, the meeting is held with the head of the Ministry of Economy and Finance, public officials from Ministries and agencies, and expert members in the Special committee on budget and accounts. The Executive branch will endeavor to justify and defend its proposed budget (Im, 2018a: 335–339).

Competition over left-over funds

Some programs may not completely be implemented or executed at a lower level than planned due to operational problems, such as weak demand or implementation problems or the exaggerated portion explained previously. In this case, the actual expenditure of the program will be less than the approved budget and the unused amount will be reported as remaining funds in the government financial report. Given the fact that the government is trying to make full use of its allocated budget to avoid future budget cuts, the presence of residual funds represents an ineffective program or a failure to implement a policy that implies a lack of demand for a particular program. Specifically, increasing or decreasing the remaining funds in the previous year will reduce or increase next year's budget. Therefore, each agency becomes busier in spending the unused funds as the end of the fiscal year approaches.

Growing left-over funds indicate the inefficiency of the programs as they are the results of lack of demand or operational problems in implementation (Kim et al., forthcoming). Kim et al., (forthcoming) have discovered that decreasing left-over funds are associated with an increasing program budget for the next fiscal year. The budget office is likely to consider a negative change in left-over funds as a product of more efficient management of a program. It then allocates more budget to the program. Presidents and politicians usually take advantage of this mechanism to expand future budget on their programs of interest. They tend to favor information that includes decreasing amount of left-over funds and ignore other information that doesn't. A similar observation can be made with different ministries because they competitively expand the budget as much as possible to avoid any future budget reduction and prove their effective use of resources.

Resource allocation: ceiling strategy for personnel

Ministries compete to recruit more personnel. However, the 'ceiling' strategy became prevalent in most personnel management departments in the public sector since 1945. The strategy limits the total number of civil servants, applying the check and balance principle to limit undue political influence over staffing and control bureaucratic expansion[2] (Choi & Jeong, 2017). The Law of General Rules on the organization and the ceiling on the number of employees were enacted under the Government Organization Act in 1977. The Korean bureaucracy has been managed based on headcounts since then.

As shown in Figure 4.4, each ministry proposes a revision of organizational structure and a new ceiling number for approval each year. At this stage, each ministry has to submit a long-term strategic plan that includes reasons for a new ceiling number. Additional supporting

Figure 4.4 Central government organizations: annual ceiling number approval process.
Source: author.

documents can be requested by the Ministry of Government Administration (MGA). Once the MGA accepts the application from each ministry, the managerial level first prescreens applications and checks requirements (Choi & Jeong, 2017). Local governments have adopted a similar process, even if they look endowed with a full autonomy in this regard. In other words, it can be said that the total number of positions of each local government is still controlled by the central government in various ways. In both the central government and local governments, the framework for inter-organizational interaction on personnel management is just like the budget game between advocates and the guardian.

The ceiling strategy originated from the concept of TO, which stands for Table of Organization. The TO of each ministry is controlled by the Division of Organization at the MGA, whose implicit mission is to prevent bureaucratic expansion. Once a position is added, the recruitment process should follow the Public Personnel Administration mandate. Ministries compete to get a larger TO by claiming that their organizations are understaffed and have heavy work overloads for their existing staff. The game between the MGA and other ministries is similar to the game between advocates and guardians in budgeting. Without a scientific measurement that gauges the appropriate size, ministries seek justifiable elements. This is when public employees like to use a popular business expression: "a crisis is an opportunity".

Most employees in ministries learn that most crises will end up with the government creating additional organizations or expanding the bureaucracy. When a scandalous incident occurs and people are angry over the government's inappropriate or inadequate responses, responsible ministries are often blamed for such wrongdoings. People harshly blame the ministry for its incompetence, insisting that the president should dismantle it or at least fire the minister. However, in reality, crises tend to result in a new organization in the ministry to prevent and deal with similar incidents in the future. Ministries can always justify their understaffing issue to the MGA and request a larger staff.

Even when no big event occurs, ministries look to expand their organization sizes. Some major tactics include establishing a subsidiary agency and absorbing it afterward; first appointing an employee in a technician position then later transferring him to an administrative position. These tactics usually precede incremental expansion of the personnel quota.

Inter-organizational policy competition

Competition among government agencies is often a jurisdictional one. As it is a competition for a policy domain, jurisdictional competition is ignited when agencies claim that a more effective policy can be implemented by transferring other agencies' functions to their jurisdiction (Im, 2018: 48). In this sense, inter-organizational competition is viewed as a struggle for policy jurisdiction, since jurisdictional competition is all about securing more budget and manpower that strengthen organizational power. Thus, increasing the policy domain is an effective device for winning in competition over limited resources. In short, policy competition is a strategy of expanding the agency's policy domain in order to hold a dominant position over other agencies. In this process, agencies produce similar policies and implementation strategies as a resolution to certain social problems, especially pending issues on which most of the public agrees that the government should take action. This section overviews several Korean examples of a bureaucratic turf war.

Local economic development policies

Rising social demand on reviving local economies, i.e. creating local jobs and providing social welfare services, emerged during the early 2000s in Korea. For example, such social pressure forced the government to push ahead with policies related to increasing the self-sustainability of rural areas and residents. Policy competition touched off by ministries such as the Ministry of Employment and Labor (MOEL), the Ministry of the Interior (MOI), and the Ministry for Food, Ministry of Agriculture, Forestry and Fisheries (MIFAFF). 'Social Enterprises', 'Community Businesses', and 'Rural Community Corporation' are some examples of names of programs that the ministries enumerated above used for stepping in a similar policy area.

The idea of sustainable growth and social entrepreneurship had started to attract attention from policymakers after the 1997 financial crisis that caused great unemployment, especially among the socially weak groups such as the elderly. This attention ultimately led to the introduction of the 'Law on the Promotion of Social Entrepreneurship' in 2007. The law originally aimed at supporting the development of small businesses and introduced a legal status for social enterprises. A social enterprise is defined by 'Korea Social Enterprise Promotion Agency (KoSEA)', which is an institute under the umbrella of MOEL, as "a company or organization which performs business activities while putting a priority on the pursuit of social purposes". Social enterprises can obtain certification only through the coordination by MOEL and KoSEA. There are now (as of July 2018) nearly 2,000 social enterprises in Korea. The graph shows that the number of operating businesses has been steadily growing ever since its launch in 2007 (Table 4.3).

Table 4.3 Number of social enterprises in Korea

Year	'07	'08	'09	'10	'11	'12	'13	'14	'15	'16	'17	'18
Certificated	55	166	77	216	155	142	269	265	295	265	256	125
Maintained	36	116	60	152	119	126	221	234	275	258	256	125
Accumulated	36	152	212	364	483	609	830	1064	1339	1597	1853	1978

Source: Korea Social Enterprise Promotion Agency (KoSEA).

Shortly after MOEL initiated the social enterprise policy, MOIS also launched a similar policy focused on creating jobs by fostering 'Community Business (CB)', which is a policy in succession to the former 'Sustainable Growth of Local Community Businesses' initiated in 2010. CB refers to businesses which are based on well-known local products or resources (e.g. locality, culture, natural resources, etc.), accountable to their community and generating positive local impacts through profits. Therefore, CBs are locally rooted, trading for the benefit of the local community, and have broad community impact as a whole. According to MOEL's 'Code of Practice and Guidance on CB', the main purpose of CB was to come up with an effective alternative to the so-called economic problem of 'growth-without-jobs' since the 1997 financial crisis, and also depart from the overly government-dependent traditional model of CB. As in the case of social enterprises, the accumulated number of CB has been increasing since 2010.

Another policy quite similar to CB and social enterprise is the 'Rural Community Corporation (RCP)' policy initiated in 2010 by MIFAFF. The primary goal of the policy was to boost local economies by inducing residents' voluntary participation in utilizing local resources through a corporate management style, ultimately generating more income and developing the community. Social conditions that gave momentum to such a policy are the increasing awareness of rural issues among urban residents, along with the impending retirement-rush of baby-boomers; nearly half of urban dwellers responded that they are interested in returning to farming after retirement (Korea Rural Economic Institute, 2015) (Table 4.4).

As seen in three cases, ministries competitively expand their policy domain under the name of enhancing local economies. The main purposes, strategies, subsidies, and contents have a considerable degree of overlap. Such overlapping roots in jurisdictional competition to win over other ministries in the bureaucratic turf war. The three cases show how policy competition among agencies heightens when certain social issues arise. It is needless to say that each agency claims a credit of the policy effects of which they have implemented.

Table 4.4 Amount of budget spent on Rural Community Corporation (RCP) (in million KRW)

Year	2011	2012	2013	2014	2015	Total
Amount of support	493	2,351	2,773	2,129	2,056	9,802

E-government turf war: MIC vs MOI

It is obvious that the driving force behind Korea transforming into a world-leading e-government country is the central government's active policies toward ICT. According to UN E-Government Development Index 2016 (EGDI),[3] Korea ranked third among 193 countries around the world, just behind the United Kingdom (first) and Australia (second). Korea has previously ranked first for three consecutive years (2010, 2012, 2014), and e-government is now one of the most valuable core competencies of the country, heavily impacting government competitiveness. However, fierce competition among government agencies regarding e-government policies has taken place ever since the government pushed ahead with e-government plans. Particularly, intense conflicts occurred between the 'Ministry of Information and Communication (MIC)' and the 'Ministry of Interior (MOI)' during President Roh's term (Yoo & Yoon, 2006).

What are the main causes of conflicts between MIC and MOI? As expected, it is all about a bureaucratic turf war, i.e. a struggle for more jurisdiction. Along with the rapid development of ICT, the degree of social impact and scope of application of technologies become increasingly unpredictable, which makes it even harder to divide jurisdiction among government agencies merely by its structure and traditional functions. So then, the first reason would be attributed to a political factor: functional restructuring of agencies. Government reforms often accompany presidential elections, for example, President Kim Dae-jung (1998–2003) and President Roh Moo-hyun (2003–2008). As a matter of fact, these are results of settling policy competitions among ministries. One of the major changes regarding ICT policies was the transfer of the initiative in e-government from MIC to MOI; the president gave a direct instruction that MOI should lead e-government policies, while MIC should support technological matters.

Another factor that intensified the fight is attributed to institutional factors: the amendment of Government Organizational Act (GOA) included many ambiguous terms. While the GOA specified that MOI takes the initiative in "general tasks related with e-government", the 'scope' of tasks related with e-government left plenty of room for interpretation, leading to jurisdictional overlapping between MOI and MIC. Not surprisingly, MOI interpreted 'scope' as wide as possible in order to maximize its jurisdiction, while MIC interpreted e-government as a subordinate of national informatization in an attempt to keep MOI in check and maintain its leading role in e-government policies.

In order to become the winner of the desperate power struggle, both MOI and MIC tried to maximize their organizational size and functions. MOI established an 'e-Government Bureau' and established three more divisions in charge of budgeting, supporting government projects, all of which are tasks transferred from MIC. Afterward, MOI expanded the 'e-Government Bureau' to 'e-Government Headquarters', and dispersed policies related to e-government throughout the whole organization. In the meanwhile, MIC maintained the 'Informatization Planning Office', although most of its functions (e.g. planning, implementation, and management related with e-government) were transferred to MOI. Instead, MIC expanded the division to a larger 'Future Information Strategy Headquarter', just as MOI have done. In order to attract political support from the media, each ministry gained an advantage over opinion leaders including reporters and scholars. For instance, MOI-held seminars and workshops consisting only of 'pro-MOI' people. In response to such strategies, MIC also endeavored to form favorable public opinions by organizing policy advisory/evaluation committee members with experts from institutes such as 'National Information Society Agency', 'Korea Agency for Digital Opportunity and Promotion', 'Korea Information Society Development Institute', and 'Electronics and Telecommunications Research Institute', all of which are affiliated organizations of MIC.

The fierce competition between MOI and MIC over jurisdictional boundaries of e-government policies during President Roh's term is a good example of a Korean bureaucratic turf war. Such inter-organizational competition is ever-present. Although the negative aspects of excessive competition and overlapping functions are summed up to a single word, 'inefficiency', it is hard to deny that there are also positive functions of competition when taking into account how much progress Korea has made in e-government. Nevertheless, one thing important in preventing competition from falling into an undesirable mud-sliding is the presence of a coordinator that actually functions. Although there were coordinating organizations such as 'e-Government Innovation Committee' or 'National Informatization Committee', it was hardly effective in most cases; after all, the president had to coordinate conflicts in many cases of jurisdictional conflicts. In this sense, the absence of an effective coordinator heavily contributes to the Korean styled 'presidential monarchy'. In short, from this case, it is plausible to come to a tentative conclusion that competition made an overall positive impact in the development of e-government but also brought about inefficiency in the process of carrying out the agencies' strategies to become the winner of the power struggle.

Consequences of organizational competition for more power

The relationship among central ministries was designed as 'equality' to generate checks and balances on the one hand and specialization for the given organizational mission(s). However, the power struggle explained earlier, just like every other form of competition, results in inequality among agencies. Back in Korean history, the origin of this competition, or superiority, can be attributed to the impetus of the country's economic growth.

Johnson (1982: 197–198) elaborated a theory to explain the Japanese economic miracle by emphasizing the role of the Ministry of International Trade and Industry. A similar story can be told about Korean economic growth. The Economic Planning Board (EPB) was the most important government department to explain Korea's economic development policy. It has been a veteran of economic policy in the Korean government for 33 years until its dissolution in 1994.

How to grow a country's economy, or to overcome poverty has been the most important problem especially for the government of a developing country. This was even truer in the military regime that ruled over Korea's rapid economic development starting in the 1960s, as it promised to take care of people's hunger. In other words, economic growth was the most satisfying gift the government could give to its people, at the cost of the regime's controversial legitimacy. It is not surprising to date the birth of EPB to July 1961, two months after the military regime's coup. EPB, which was in the form of the budget department combined with the Ministry of Finance, started with much autonomy (Kwon, 2017: 36). Ruined by harsh Japanese colonial exploitation and the Korean War (1950–1953), Korea lacked an adequate amount of capital, technology, and skilled labor that were required to develop the economy. In this context, EPB played a locomotive role in getting foreign aid and loans as well as learning technology by purchasing machines from abroad to nurture Korean industries. Not having an affluent class and a mature market, EPB was endowed with all the power necessary for achieving the national goal without any external constraint such as market resistance, labor unions, etc. This full autonomy meant independent and autonomous positions and reduced working constraints from other stakeholders in the same field.

The president's preoccupation with economic growth gave substantial power to EPB. Such power guaranteed EPB a far superior position to other ministries such as the Ministry of Commerce and Industry or the Ministry of Agriculture. The EPB's superiority pertains to its legal status within the government. Upon its establishment, the EPB's head was given the same status as a minister. As the president recognized the coordination problem inside the government, the rank of the EPB's head soon escalated to a deputy prime minister in December 1963. This means that the EPB minister had a higher status and could exercise higher legal executive rights than other ministers.

Relying on its power of budget allocation and planning over other ministries, the EPB increasingly expanded the size of its organization and further extended its policy territory to diverse areas. In Korea, the ministry related to economic affairs has been the winner of the inter-agency competition, enjoying the sweet reign of autonomy – the result of a power game in organizational competitions.

The winners obtain a great amount of power, while losers obtain fear of abolition and need for keeping the status quo. In other words, although it is a common sense that a discrepancy of power is ubiquitous within central government agencies, it is quite challenging to clearly discern power differences among different organizations.

Power, a highly ambiguous and context-oriented concept, is difficult to measure or quantify. However, several studies (Oh, 2006, 2013, 2018) have tackled the challenge, operationalizing 'bureaucratic power' as a composite of an agency's resources, autonomy, network, organizational slacks, and potentials. Table 4.5 shows the ten most powerful agencies of previous three administrations, based on the bureaucratic power index (BPI).

As predicted, agencies such as the 'Ministry of Finance and Strategy (present Ministry of Economy and Finance, MOEF)' and 'Supreme Prosecutors' Office (SPO)' turn out to be the most powerful agencies during all three administrations. Most of the top-ranked agencies are *Bu* organizations, while lower rank agencies are mostly *Cheo* and *Cheong* organizations. However, there are some exceptions: 'Supreme Prosecutors' Office' (*Cheong*), 'National Police Agency' (*Cheong*), 'National Intelligence Service' (*Won*), and the 'Board of Audit and Inspection' (*Won*). These are examples of winners in the competition game.

However, the fact that most of the top ten powerful agencies are *Bu* organizations does not necessarily mean that all Bu organizations are the center of power. The power gap turns out to be huge even among Bu organizations; agencies such as the 'Ministry of Gender Equality and Family' and the 'Ministry of SMEs and Startups' are ranked as some of the weakest agencies, despite their status as *Bu* organizations. Another observation, interestingly, is that *Bu* organizations that hold a subordinate *Cheong* organization.[4] This supports the common sense shared by Korean civil servants: "big equals power". Holding a

Table 4.5 The ten most powerful government organizations for the three previous administrations

	Roh Moo-hyun (2003–2008)	Lee Myung-bak (2008–2013)	Park Geun-hye (2013–2017)
1	Ministry of Finance and Economy	Ministry of Strategy and Finance	Ministry of Strategy and Finance
2	Ministry of National Defense	Supreme Prosecutors' Office	Supreme Prosecutors' Office
3	Supreme Prosecutors' Office	Ministry of National Defense	Ministry of National Defense
4	Ministry of Education and Human Resources Development	Ministry of Land, Transport and Maritime Affairs	Ministry of Land, Infrastructure, and Transport
5	Ministry of Construction and Transportation	Ministry of Education, Science, and Technology	Ministry of Trade, Industry, and Energy
6	Ministry of Commerce Industry and Energy	Ministry of the Interior and Safety	Ministry of Education
7	Ministry of the Interior	National Intelligence Service	National Intelligence Service
8	Ministry of Foreign Affairs and Trade	Ministry of Knowledge Economy	Ministry of the Interior
9	Ministry of Health and Welfare	Ministry of Foreign Affairs and Trade	National Police Agency
10	National Police Agency	Board of Audit and Inspection	Ministry of Health and Welfare

Source: Oh (2013, 2018).

subordinate *Cheong* increases the satisfaction of *Bu* employees since *Cheong* is often exploited as a means of alleviating personnel congestion by taking in high officials from the parent *Bu* organization. In addition, "Parachutes", a jargon for these circumstances, has prevailed upon the bureaucratic expansion in Korea over the years.

Interbranch competition: executive-legislative relations

This chapter has introduced some concrete examples of competition among agencies within the Korean executive branch. The phenomenon of competition among agencies can be also found elsewhere, even between the executive and legislative branches. In a broad associative definition, a government in general consists of a legislature, executive, and judiciary branch. Thus, all three branches should function properly. Particularly, considering that public service is effective only when both legislation and execution are carried out properly, forming a healthy parliament-executive (competitive) relationship is pivotal in a democratic country. This section goes through how the relationship between the two branches has changed since the establishment of the Korean government in 1948 and offers a diagnosis of the current status.

The history of the Korean government, since its establishment in the middle of the chaos of 1948, is summed as a history of amending deficiencies of the perfunctorily introduced Western-style political system of representative democracy. In the early period of the developmental era, the parliament was unable to fulfill its duty of keeping the executive branch in check, due to the low political culture. The people were not yet familiar with democratic culture such as political participation. In particular, the presidents who were former generals viewed the Western-oriented democracy did not fit with Korean culture. They would rather run an authoritarian government, except for the Second Republic.[5] The parliament has ever since struggled to secure its position as an independent institute, autonomous from the president and executive branch.

Parliamentary privilege has shrunk during the authoritarian regimes of President Park Chung-hee (1961–1979), President Chun Doo-hwan (1981–1988), and President Roh Tae-woo (1988–1993). Even if the Korean Constitution had adopted a presidential system, both executive and legislative branches could propose bills to the parliament. The number of bills reflects their respective institutional powers because preparing a bill requires time and specialty.

Kim (2017)'s study shows that the executive branch wielded more power over the legislative branch in terms of a number of legislative bills until the 15th National Assembly Term,[6] except for during the sixth term (1963–1967). The number has reversed since the 2000s, meaning that the parliament began to function as a legislator. Concomitantly, the function of keeping the executive and presidential powers in check has also increased, somewhat alleviating the drawbacks of the so-called "presidential monarchy"; the president can no longer wield absolute power over the parliament, nor does the majority party have the president at its beck and call.

It is easy to imagine how the parliament was suppressed under the autocratic state. The ruling party became virtually a rubber stamp for passing bills in the Congress, while opposition parties took actions of convening intellectuals and the working class, which had little impact on increasing parliamentary autonomy. However, along with the collapse of authoritarian governments and dispersion of pro-democratic values, the parliament began to start functioning as an autonomous institute. Along with the power shifts from conservative to liberal (1997) and vice versa (2007), the ruling party is no longer always the majority party, increasing the political control of the parliament. The number of laws proposed by the legislative/executive branch is a good indicator of the power relationships of the two branches.

To cut straight to the point, the initial form of Korean democracy was based on an executive branch that was more competitive than the legislative branch (Im, 2018). The de facto hierarchy between the two branches during the authoritarian regimes has changed as democracy matured. Checks and balances of the Congress did not exist in the earlier authoritarian periods, but the legislative branch increasingly gained power to exercise controls on the executive branch.

Concluding remarks

This chapter intends to bridge the gap between competition within organizations and competition between different organizations. In doing so, the first section of the chapter is reserved to reveal how an organization's operation mechanism may lead to competition with other organizations. The discussion begins with a typical collective decision-making system within a government organization. *Pumyui* reflects how respective projects can be approved over its circulation throughout the hierarchical bureaucracy. After a brief introduction of the Korean government structure, a thorough examination of central government ministries and executive-legislative relations elaborates on how inter-organizational competition is represented in the public sector. Bureaucratic expansion, leadership in policy implementation, and budget maximization are all prevailing forms of competition among different organizations. Regionalism in Chapter 5 will extend the analysis of inter-organizational competition to local-local relations and central-local relations.

Notes

1 The final budget plan will be reviewed through the *pumyui* process within the ministry before it is submitted to the guardian.
2 Ceilings have been frequently used to keep government employment constant. Organization size became a critical issue in public administration after World War II (Light, 1999).

3 The EGDI is a composite measure of three important dimensions of e-government, namely: provision of online services, telecommunication connectivity, and human capacity. It is reported by UN on a biennial basis.
4 Are more powerful than those without. For example, the Ministry of Finance and Strategy holds SUB-organizations such as 'National Tax Service', 'Korea Customs Service', 'Public Procurement Service', and 'Statistics Korea'. The Ministry of National Defense holds 'Military Manpower Administration' and 'Defense Acquisition Program Administration', all of which are subordinate Cheong organizations.
5 The Second Republic of Korea, which lasted for eight months (June 15, 1960– May 16, 1961), was the only government under a parliamentary system in the history of the Korean government.
6 As mentioned in the earlier section, ministries typed as a Bu organization have legislative powers, which is pivotal in power struggle among agencies within the executive branch.

References

Cho, S. (1984). The pumyui system and the decision-making process of Korean administration (in Korean). *Korean Journal of Public Administration*, 22(1), 112–115.

Cho, S., & Im, T. (2016). *Korean Public Organization Theories* (in Korean). Paju: Bobmunsa.

Choi, H., & Jeong, J. (2017). The ceiling strategy as policy: Limiting bureaucratic expansion and democratization. In Im, T. (Ed.). *The Experience of Democracy and Bureaucracy in South Korea* (pp. 217–240). West Yorkshire: Emerald Publishing Limited.

Crozier, M. (1964). *Bureaucratic Phenomenon*. Chicago: Chicago University Press.

Im, T. (2010). *Korean Administrative Organization Theory*. Paju, Korea: Bobmoonsa.

Im, T. (2011). Information technology and organizational morphology: The case of the Korean central government. *Public Administration Review*, 71(3), 435–443.

Im, T. (2014). Organizational changes in the Korean central government: Historical perspective (in Korean). *Korean Review of Organizational Studies*, 11(1), 1–45.

Im, T. (2016). *Public Organizations in Asia*. New York: Routledge.

Im, T. (2018a). *Public Administration* (in Korean). Seoul: Pakyoungsa.

Im, T. (2018b). Towards a more matured representative democracy: An analysis of government-legislature relations (in Korean). *Korean Journal of Public Administration*, 27(2), 1–35.

Johnson, C. (1982). *MITI and the Japanese Miracle: The Growth of Industrial Policy, 1925–1975*. Stanford, CA: Stanford University Press.

Kim, B. W. et al. (forthcoming). Unused funds and budget decision: Rationality or Bureaucratic Self Interest? (*Journal Unknown*).

Kim, D. R. (2017). Executive-legislative competition in agenda setting: an analysis of longitudinal changes in South Korea. *Asian Journal of Political Science*, 25(3): 383–400.

Kim, K. S. (2000). An empirical study on state functions and administrative tools in the Korean Central Government. *Korean Public Administration Review*, 34(1), 59–81.

Korea Rural Economic Institute. (2015). *How to Develop 6th Industralization Skilled Workforces.* Naju, Korea: Korea Rural Economic Institute.

Kwon, H. (2017). Leaving behind the developmental state: The changing rationale of governance in Korean governments. In Choi, J., Kwon, H., & Koo, M. G. (Eds.). *The Korean Government and Public Policies in a Development Nexus: Sustaining Development and Tackling Policy Changes – Vol. 2* (p. 36). New York: Springer.

Lee, S., & Oh, S. (2014). Research on functions and limitations of Korean "Cheong" organizations (in Korean). *Korean Journal of Public Administration*, 23(3), 81–110.

Light, P. C. (1999). *The True Size of Government.* Washington, D.C.: Brookings Institution Press.

Min, J. (2006). A study on the organizational change in Korean central government agency. *Korean Society and Public Administration*, 17(2), 1–23.

Oh, J. R. (2006). Bureaucratic power: Conceptualization, operationalization and measurement model. *Korean Public Administration Review*, 40(4), 377–400.

Oh, J. R. (2013). Developing and validating concepts and measures of bureaucratic power in Korean Central Government. *Korean Journal of Public Administration*, 51(1), 31.

Oh, J. R. (2018). Measuring bureaucratic power: Focusing on the central administration agencies in Korea. *Korean Public Administration Review*, 52(1), 139–166.

Rosenberg, D., & Tomkins, C. (1983). The budget liaison officer in local government—Guardian or advocate? *Local Government Studies*, 9(5), 51–64.

Selznick, P. (1948). Foundations of the theory of organization. *American Sociological Review*, 13(1), 25–35.

Tsai, W. (2002). Social structure of "coopetition" within a multiunit organization: Coordination, competition, and intraorganizational knowledge sharing. *Organization Science*, 13(2), 179–190.

Yoo, H. R., & Yoon, S. O. (2006). Analysis of conflicts among ministries in the e-government promotion process: Focusing on the conflict between Ministry of Interior and Ministry of Information and Communication. *Journal of Korean Policy Studies*, 10(4), 397–420.

Wildavsky, A. (1975). *Budgeting: A Comparative Theory of Budgetary Processes.* Boston/Toronto: Little Brown and Company.

5 Governance from the competition perspective

This chapter further examines Korea's unique cultural competition factors, such as familism and collectivism from previous chapters, with respect to Korea's regional characteristic being the unit of analysis. This chapter widens the scope of analysis to the country level using competitive trait to explain political space of governance in Korea.

Regionalism: factors segregated regional ideology

Overview of geographical context

South Korea has two levels of the local administrative government system. The first level is local government at regional-scale and the other is local government at city-scale that deals with street-level policy implication. The regional-scale administrative division is called *do*, which is similar to the meaning of "province", and there are eight provinces in Korea (Gyeonggi-do,, Gangwon-do, Chungcheongnam(south)-do, Chungcheongbuk(north)-do, Jeollanam(south)-do, Jeollabuk(north)-do, Gyeongsangnam(south)-do, and Gyeongsangbuk(north)-do), one autonomous province (Jeju-do), and one special city (Seoul). In general, the capital region indicates Seoul and Gyeonggi-do, the central region as Gangwon-do, Chungcheongnam (south)-do and Chungcheongbuk (north)-do, the Southwest region as Jeollanam (south)-do and Jeollabuk (north)-do, and Southeast region as Gyeongsangnam (south)-do and Gyeongsangbuk (north)-do. Due to the geographical characteristics of Korea – where the east is mountainous, while the west is full of plains – the Southwest region historically had been the one rich in agricultural resources. In contrast, the Southwest region has never been fully developed in terms of agriculture, and thus, resources and wealth were relatively more scarce in the Southwest region than in the Southeast (Figure 5.1).

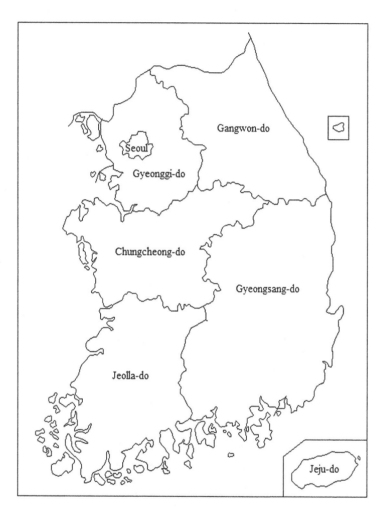

Figure 5.1 Map of Korea.

Region as unit of competition: **jibang**

The capital area centering in Seoul has functioned as the major region since the Chosun dynasty (1392–1910). The Chosun dynasty was the last kingdom before the establishment of the Republic of Korea. Functioning as the center of administration, politics, and economy, Seoul rapidly developed and urbanized during the country's industrialization process. Consequentially, the gap between urban and rural areas began to widen rapidly. There was an influx of migrants coming from various rural regions to Seoul wishing to find a sufficient job, especially during the industrialization period.

As a consequence, Seoul experienced rapid urbanization, marketization, and Westernization. Housing and living costs in Seoul also rose quickly. After the Korean War, there was no longer a social class in Korea in the strict sense of the term. However, since all aspects of economic, political, and social infrastructure and resources were concentrated in Seoul, living in Seoul was the new prestige. In contrast, all areas except Seoul remained predominantly agricultural. All non-Seoul areas were called *jibang*, which meant "anywhere other than Seoul". Seoul-*jibang* became the Korean version of the dichotomous relationship of urban-rural and center-countryside. Therefore, young people who are born in the non-Seoul area still aspire to live in Seoul even these days. These social phenomena during urbanization and the developmental era are accumulated to form regionalism.

Historical factors: strong central government, weak regionalism

In order to understand province-based regionalism, one needs to understand the situation in the Chosun dynasty first. During the Chosun era, the king clearly defined and divided administrative districts by law and established a centralized ruling system. Bureaucrats from the central government were selected and assigned to each province by the king. Even during that time, each province had a slightly different culture and different ways to survive based on geographical context and climate. However, these differences did not function as the driving force for political unity. Indeed, regionalism in Korea has been different from regionalism in the West. Regionalism in Western countries occurs naturally through the difference in religions, languages, and races. However, Korea is historically governed as one nation with one ethnic group and a single language. In other words, Korea's regionalism is not caused by 'natural' differences. Korean regionalism has been artificially formed, expanded, and reproduced through development and democratization.

Economic factors: state-led development and regional disparities during industrialization

It is widely known that spatial division in Korea is also closely related to the state's economic development strategy. From the 1960s to the 1980s, the economy was prioritized in all policy areas. Since the market was not fully developed to become the economic driver, the Korean government established the 'Economic Planning Board' to take that role. When the government allocated resources such as infrastructure or industrial complexes and facilities, they based their location decision on the economy, not fairness, causing uneven regional development. The economic development of Korea in the 1970s focused on industrializing the core, central region while sacrificing the rural sphere area due to limited resources. During the beginning of the 1970s, the government's official slogan of modernization was maintained, and public support was gained. There was a consensus that even if only a specific region was to be developed, if it would profit the country, then it would mean profit for all citizens.

Economic development was done in conjunction with regional development under the National Land Comprehensive Plan, which had been in operation since 1972. The First National Land Comprehensive Development Plan aimed at establishing infrastructure for high economic growth and development. As a result, the almost city-scale new industrial complex was constructed in the Southeast region, followed by a number of multi-purpose dams and the Gyeongbu Expressway. The Ulsan Industrial Complex is a representative example.

The government invested 7.7% of the total investment in the first five-year economic development plan to the Southeastern region. If one is to make a calculation only in the industrial sector, 24.8% of the total investment was invested solely in the Ulsan Industrial Center. Later on, the government felt the limits of light industry in the 1970s, and pursued a heavy chemical industrial strategy as a key strategy for export. At that time, the government developed the heavy chemical industry centered on the Ulsan Industrial Complex again.

By contrast, the Southwest and Gangwon region witnessed stagnation or decline in their economies. According to the Gwangju City Editorial Committee (1995: 525–526), there had been little improvement to the manufacturing infrastructure in Gwangju city – the capital city of Southwest region – even after the liberation from Japan.[1] This shows that the industrialization of certain regions, such as the Southwest, was delayed because the government focused mainly on the Southeast region. This consequential gap in economic development then became a factor of regionalism and regional competitiveness.

Political factor: local communities and regional political party

The regional disparity in elite recruitment is another factor pointed out as the background of Korean regionalism. Statistics also show that there is a gap in the composition of the group of the economically dominant in Korea. Whether it is the elite recruitment, or wealth distribution being concentrated in one area, people outside of the beneficiary region feel they are discriminated against. Because of such sentiment may arouse a sense of identifying oneself to their place, leading to the intensification of regionalism, whether such a gap is true or not is important.

Let us first look at the distribution of government elites by region. The ratio of the ministers appointed by President Park Chung-hee and the 1970's population ratio by the administrative districts are summarized as follows (Table 5.1).

If we tie Gyeonggi-do to Seoul, concerning minister positions, one can say that they have recruited talented people fairly from each region. Nevertheless, in the case of the economic elite represented by the Chaebol (Owner of major conglomerate), the situation is reversed as shown in Table 5.2.

In the course of Korea's state-led economic growth, conglomerates were given birth to by the state and functioned as a subordinate to state power. This is because conglomerates grew up with state instruction and

Table 5.1 Ministers of Park Chung-hee regime

	Minister	*1970's population ratio*
Seoul	18.8	17.5
Gyeonggi-do	5.7	10.7
Central region	17.1	13.8
Southeast region	31.3	30.4
Southwest region	21.4	20.4
Gangwon and Jeju	5.7	6.6

Source: Modified from Choi (1999: 106).
Excluding those who migrated from the North Korean province (21.1% of the total).

Table 5.2 Distribution of 1960 Chaebol by region

	Chaebol	*1970's population ratio*
Seoul and Gyeonggi-do	17.7	28.2
Central region	13.9	13.8
Southeast region	50.6	30.4
Southwest region	11.4	20.4
Gangwon do	6.3	6.6

Source: Modified from Choi (1999: 106).
Excluding those who migrated from the North Korean province (21.1% of the total).

selective support rather than market competition. So, under the precondition where the Chaebol is equivalent to economic elites, it becomes obvious there is a visible regional difference regarding who could gain wealth and who could not. Thus, it would be very naïve to say there has been no regional gap in terms of elite recruitment just because the above administrative bureaucratic distribution appears equally.

One inference to be made here is that a considerable number of entrepreneurs from the Southeast region – those who were born in the process of national industrialization in the 1960s – can be deduced, and an amazingly low number of entrepreneurs from Southwest region are observed when compared to their population ratio. Moreover, except for the Southeast and Southwest regions, the presence of economic elites is distributed according to the population proportion. However, the Southwest region has relatively fewer economic elites than its population proportion, whereas the Southeast region has a number of entrepreneurs that is almost a twofold amount of its population proportion.[2]

As mentioned earlier, the Southwest region was rich in agricultural resources and there were many agricultural-based landowners in the past. However, in the process of land reforms of the President Rhee Syng-man (the first president of the Republic of Korea), the existing agrarian economic elite – the landowning class – collapsed and the number of yeomen farmers increased. Although the collapsed landowners grew more dependent on government support, being unable to turn themselves into entrepreneurs without support from the state, there was little aid from the government.

Park Chung-hee regime's concentrated industrialization in the Southeast region enabled the region to achieve rapid economic growth, although the region lacked agricultural assets. In fact, as of 1963, the gross regional product (GRP) income of residents in the Southeast region was the lowest in the country. Even the GRP of the northern area of the Southeast region was 13% lower than that of the northern area of Southwest region. Through selective industrialization, the economic level of the Southeast region in the 1970s far exceeded other regions.[3] In sum, the poorest region in the country developed into one of the wealthiest regions in less than a decade. The region became a strong support base for Park Chung-hee, which will be discussed later.

Political factor: regionalism and party politics

Since the central province is composed of newly moved people, regionalism is not so strong. On the other hand, the community of the other eight, non-central provinces (called *jibang*) is tied to local politics. Especially, uneven development among eight provinces triggered regionalism. In some provinces, government-led development amplified the growth of the local economy and residents gained wealth through housing and land price increases. These regions were more likely to support the president. On the other hand, provinces with no government support had to watch their neighboring region's growth. They were less likely to support the president. In order to have resources from the government, they had a strong bond to elect a president who can allocate more resources to their province. Thus, the president's regional background becomes a critical criteria rather than election promises in voters' decision.

The study on the effects of the state on regional development shows that 78.6% of the research's respondents think that regional development is influenced by the regional connection of political power.[4] This is based on the economic supremacy of the region selected in the industrialization process and the inequality of the region not selected in the industrialization process. The beginning of competition between political parties based on regionalism was the 1963 presidential election. It can be seen from the fact that Park Chung-hee emphasized his regional origin from the Southeast region in order to get voting power from the Southeast, which had the largest population at that time. The article "The winner is the loser, the loser is the winner" of *Chosun Ilbo* (the top newspaper and now the largest media corporation in Korea) on October 18, 1963, quoted the phrase, "Lead the native of Yeongnam to the presidency". Considering that the voting house of the Southeast region used to be set as a local issue, the 1963 presidential election can be regarded as the beginning of regionalism in the political sphere. Still, at this moment there were relatively few regional conflict factors.

The political expression of regional emotion was invented in the mid-1960s. From this point on, local feelings became the main sentiment – a sense of unity and belonging – among those living in the Southeast region and became a key factor as a social bond among them. Then this emotion developed into Korean familism. However, the issue of uneven development and economic superiority in the Southeast was raised, especially when the election was held. Local mass media continuously wrote articles pointing out the central government's attitude toward this region. Furthermore, a special organization called "Jeollanam-do inhospitality rectify committee" was established that called for the abolition of discrimination against Jeollanam-do (southern area of Southwest region). This organization put pressure on the government on the policy alienation of Jeollanam-do and actively lobbied the government.

The issue of a double-track on the Southwest railway was the reason for a hostile discourse started in Jeollanam-do – again the southern region of the Southwest – that expanded to the whole of Southwest region. The promise to change the Southwest Line railway, which was a single line, to a double line had been overturned for decades since the liberation. This was because of the competitiveness of Seoul and the Yeongnam regions, which had become industrialized due to the unbalanced industrialization economic policy.

Kim Dae-jung, then the opposing politician to Park Chung-hee, strongly argued to improve the competitiveness of the Southwest region and for changes in the existing authoritarian political system. So, he was able to get strong support of Southwest residents. With the emergence of Kim Dae-jung, a rivalry has begun to form between the Southwest regional political party centered on Kim Dae-jung and the Southeast regional political party which supported the existing regime and Park Chung-hee. In other words, the regional discrimination theory and the competition to be an economically developed area led to a regional party competition in the political sphere.

In the 1971 presidential election, Kim Dae-jung embarked on the slogan of "10 years of rotten politics, I cannot stand more, let's change!" This slogan reflected the atmosphere of Korean society in which regional conflicts were exposed at the time and the social conflicts that had been inherent in authoritarian nationalism due to the economic crisis surfaced. As a result, in the 1971 presidential election, Kim Dae-jung who officially obtained 5.39 million votes proved to be a threatening political rival to Park Chung-hee who earned 6.34 million votes despite his incumbent advantage. Consequently, the New Democratic Party, which Kim Dae-jung was headed at the time, was able to make a political leap forward in opposition to the ruling party.

At the time of the presidential election, local conflicts between the two regions were at the peak. In response to the Kim Dae-jung and the Southwest regional political party, the Southeast regional political party spread the "President Silla" (the kingdom that ruled the Southeast region in the Middle Ages old Korea peninsula) discourse. Even at that time, the National Intelligence Agency spread a false leaflet saying that people in the Southwest decided to boycott the Southeast's goods for three days before the election. Therefore, residents of the Southeast region, who were already enjoying regional superiority and familism, felt a consciousness of crisis that they could lose their vested rights when the regime changed and gathered as a candidate for Park Chung-hee. Also consequently, Park Chung-hee, who felt threatened by the presidential election in 1971, eventually started a dictatorship regime called the Yushin regime. As the Yushin regime entered, Kim Dae-jung went into exile to the United States while fighting against the Yushin regime.

After the assassination of Park Chung-hee by his subordinate Kim Jae-gyu in 1979, a new military government was formed through the 12.12 coup d'état. In the democratization forces, Kim Dae-jung again arose as a politician representing democracy and the Southwest region together with another popular democratic politician Kim Yong-sam representing the Southeast. Moreover, the military group cruelly suppressed many citizens by putting the army into the Southwest on May 18 in 1980 to stop the democratization movement in Gwangju, a large city in the Southwest region. So, their oppression in Gwangju furthered the democratic/anti-democratic composition of the regional emotions that had been built up due to imbalanced development. These regional emotions were expressed by the competitiveness between local representative political parties in the Southeast region and Southwest region through voting.

Political regionalism: voting behavior

Region as the concept of 'Family'

After the coup, the nation-wide resistance to the Chun Doo-hwan regime continued. In 1987, Chun finally gave up his power and the democratization of Korea began. However, in the 1987 presidential election after democratization, Kim Young-sam and Kim Dae-jung became political rivals showing the fierce competition of regional political parties.

In the first direct election to elect a president since the democratization in 1987, there was a failure to unify candidates between Kim Young-sam and Kim Dae-jung. For an election victory, Kim Dae-jung at the time wanted to remove his progressive image by putting forth as passive response about the ideological dispute. On the other hand, Kim Young-sam's camp has been more assertive about the issue of ending military government and democratization. As a result, democracy became a policy rift between the candidates Kim Dae-jung and Kim Young-sam. Not surprisingly, the votes of the people who expected democratization were divided. And Roh Tae-woo, a former general who was a member of the previous military government, was elected. Although the competition of the two political figures developed Korean political party politics, it also tarnished the meaning of democratization that the people gained by the struggle with the new military government.

Even in the 1991 presidential election, regionalism exerted its influence again. Kim Young-sam cooperated with Roh Tae-woo in order to win over Kim Dae-jung, who was supported by the Southwest and ran for the presidential election with three parties. At a restaurant called *Chowon Bokjip*, Kim Young-sam's close supporters including a public prosecutor said, "We are family, let's fall off the Yeongdo Bridge and die if we lose the election". The People's Party, which was an opposition party, wiretapped and disclosed the remarks. This was an exemplary case, demonstrating regionalism in favor of the Southeast region, which has been supported by both the northern and southern areas of the Southeast. The revelations about the *Chowon Bokjip* scandal, which incited regionalism, backfired on Southeast region votes. It was more problematic that the behavior of the political party that encouraged regional sentiments, rather than the course of exposing the scandal. Moreover, the *Chowon Bokjip* dialogue drew competition based on the nepotism and superiority of the entire Southeast region.

Kim Young-sam, who stimulated regionalism in the entire Southeast with 9.9 million votes, became the president of the Republic of Korea with a difference of 1.9 million votes from Kim Dae-jung. In the 1997 presidential election, Kim Dae-jung cooperated with Kim Jong-pil, who represented the central region. Kim Jong-pil was the prime-minister during the Park Chung-hee regime and he also stimulated central region's regionalism by saying the "Central region is no pushover". Finally, Kim Dae-jung won the election with 40.3% of the vote. The representative party in the Southwest region became the ruling party, and the Southeast regional ruling party became the opposition party. Roh Moo-hyun, a renowned human rights lawyer, won the presidential election in 2002. His approval rating was lower than another candidate's, But he miraculously reversed the presidential primary. It was called the "Roh wind". Regionalism also had a big influence in this election. The result that about 90% of the Southwest region voters selected Roh Moo-hyun proved the influence of regionalism in the politics area. However, the power shifted again to the Southeastern after the subsequent 2007 presidential election. President Lee Myung-bak, former CEO of Hyundai Group from the Southeast region, became the president and those of this region returned to the center of the ruling group in the political arena. Lee Myung-bak won 48.7% of the total votes, and this was 22.6% higher than the runner-up Chung Dong-young, who belonged to Southwest regional party. Chung Dong-young's approval rating in the Southwest region was then about 80%. This fact means that localized voting behavior was strongly functioning in Korea.

During the 2012 presidential election, Moon Jae-in, the political successor to Roh Moo-hyun, and Park Geun-hye, the daughter of

Park Chung-hee and his political successor, met in the presidential election. At this time, regionalism worked again, and both candidates showed overwhelming approval ratings in their respective regions. Moon Jae-in had about 80% support from the Southwest region. And Park Geun-hye also had about 80% of approval rate in the northern area of the Southeast region where she and her father Park Chung-hee came from. In the end, Park Geun-hye was elected, but Park Geun-hye was impeached with the Choi Soon-sil Scandal in 2017. In the subsequent presidential election, President Moon Jae-in argued for social reform and developed Southwest-friendly policy. Finally, he was able to win the presidential election with 41% of support.

This competition is derived from the sense of superiority of Southeast residents due to the urbanization and industrialization policies concentrated in the Southeast region and the sense of equality of Southwest residents, who were not selected in by industrialization policy. As a result, regions in Korea became families and local self-interest and regionalism always had a great influence on the presidential election. In addition, Korea's politics stimulated the competition of local residents, which enabled the attainment of formal democracy within a short period through competition and regime change among regional representative political parties. Moreover, regime change was able to balance industrialization in whole Korea region.

Decentralization

Local autonomy on the Korean Peninsula, where the history of central government is over 500 years old, was a strange concept in the first place. Thus, local autonomy in Korea began in 1996 by devolving power from top to bottom, not from the provinces to the central government, and from the bottom up. The introduction of decentralization reform, which consists of mainly introducing local elections, was difficult. Central politicians were reluctant for fear of losing their powers. The reform program was implemented slowly, but was possible because of regionalism. Regionalists, dissatisfied with relative deprivation, were eager to be empowered by the reform.

Korea's local autonomy system, which started with a power commission from the top of the central government, only changed the nomination of provincial governors and mayors, which existed in the central government, to local elections. The education superintendent has also changed from the previous appointment of the central government to the election by local residents. The creation of the local assembly has provided both a sense of equality and a sense of superiority for local residents with the aforementioned sense of regionalism. Local politics and local officials demanded that the central government be officially treated the same as if their districts were lagging behind those nearby, based on a sense of equality. At the same time, however, he called for differential support from his constituency to satisfy residents' sense of superiority. As a result, the controversy over the imbalance of support and regulation for local governments was continued by the sense of equality among local governments.

The aforementioned regionalism of Southeast region vs Southwest region was the biggest variable in the local elections. In order to win local elections, it was advantageous to run as a member of the local representative party. Korean political parties were able to expand and reproduce regionalism through nomination by controlling local government heads and local councilors. As a result, Korea's party culture has become rigid in its discipline despite its presidential system.

Regionalism has again had a huge impact on local elections. This means that the system allows for party-led local administration and local politics based on regionalism, away from administration-led local administration and local politics. Thus, the confrontation between regional and political parties intensifies the competition in the political arena (Figure 5.2).

The earlier picture is the result from the election of the head of the local governments in the local elections of 1998. Regions shaded in white are the area where the head of the metropolitan government of the Southwest regional party was elected. Regions shaded in dark grey are the area where the head of the local government of the Southeast regional party was elected (Figure 5.3).

The earlier figure is the result of the local election of the head of the metropolitan government in 2014. Regions in white represent belonging to the Southwest regional political party, and those in grey represent belonging to the Southeast political party. This example explains that local regionalism also has a great influence on local elections, especially in the Southwest region and the Southeast region.

Candlelight protests as the citizen's voice

Given that South Korea went through the development administration era with its powerful state autonomy, it seems logical that less-developed regions felt the need to make their own voice to compete for their privileged neighborhood. Otherwise, policy beneficiary group, in this case, residents in the Southeast region, would not give up their advantage voluntarily. Their voice led to the introduction of a

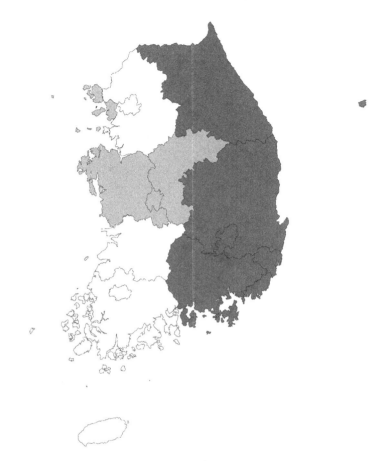

Figure 5.2 The result of the 1998 local elections.

democratic institution, but this failed to reconstruct spatially equivalent social development.

The competitive spirit at the regional level was one of the fundamental motivations that led two core democratic revolutions in South Korea, which are the June Democratic Uprising of 1987 and Candlelight Revolution of 2017. The longing for competitiveness not only made those events possible but changed the power distribution across the country after each revolution. Those two transitions were the achievements of South Korean citizens, who struggled to overcome the regionalism that has affected inequity both politically and socially. They opened a gateway to regionally fair way based in participatory democracy.

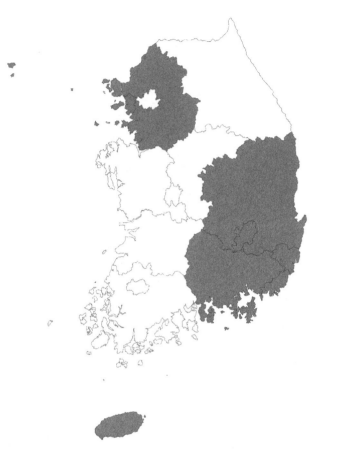

Figure 5.3 The result of the 2014 local elections.

Rural-city competition: city promotion

Decentralization triggered a micro-level regionalism under the regionalism at the macroscale explained previously. For example, rural areas compete to obtain a city status of *si*. Under *do* – the provincial government of Korea – there is a basic unit of *si* and *goon*. A *goon*, the administrative unit of non-urban areas in Korea, consists of each *uep*, which is an urban-style county and a number of *myeon* which consist of farming and fishing villages. Farmers usually live in *myeon* and usually go out to the *uep* to buy groceries for three or five days at the market. Therefore, not only is there a government office located in *uep*, but there are also stores developed as a commercial hub.

Although urban areas have many drawbacks compared to rural areas, residents of most provinces have called for the promotion to become city-level units. In particular, people who feel competitiveness to the city but cannot go to the city due to socio-economic constraints, and those who are attached to the region, strongly demand promotion to city districts. Public officials also strongly support the promotion because it will increase the number of civil servants. In order to meet the demands of this public demand, local councilors and others are pushing ahead with the promotion. In other words, minor-regionalism is strongly influenced in that it is led by those who benefit from it. As a result, the number of cities increased from 14 in 1948 to 75 in 2018.

The consequences of a city promotion can be summarized as follows: First, the ratio of the number of people in the city hall to those in the higher positions will dramatically increase. This will solve the problems of personnel congestion for promotion at once. Past examples of *uep* (town)-to-*si* (city)' promotion show that, on average, the number of civil servants has increased more than six times since the city's promotion, even if the population has changed little or even decreased.

Second, the new residents of regions that recently have moved up as a city have a high sense of superiority and unity. However, the people in nearby *goon* regions that have lost to become a city feel competitive or jealous because of the symbolic meaning of a city in Korea. So once promoted to city, *si*, it would remain as it is, but would never return to *goon* again.

Let's take a closer look at the link between promotion to *si* and the competition process. The *eup*, the most urbanized district among the rural communities in Korea, is first promoted to a city. Then, a *goon* – a lower status than *eup* – around the new city (or the formal neighboring *eup*) feels competitive and also wants the promotion. If a *goon* calls for the promotion, the government integrates *goons* nearby to become one city of 'urban and agricultural complex'. This way of managing competitiveness and the needs of residents is the most typical scene observed in the government.

Gwang-yeok si is a metropolitan municipality that has strong characteristics of urbanization. The promotion to *gwang-yeok si* has political significance similar to the promotion of the *goon* to the *si*, as explained previously. The development of a local hub city results in a concentration of population and massive urbanization. It will then be necessary to provide other administrative services. Therefore, city dwellers feel competitive about *gwang-yeok si* and want to promote it through integration between the cities.

The integration of Changwon City, Masan City, and Jinhae City is an example of consolidating neighboring cities hoping eventually to be promoted to *gwang-yeok si* in the future. The integration of Changwon City, Masan City, and Jinhae City started with a policy of abolishing provinces, integrating cities and counties, and transforming the entire nation into more than 60 metropolitan cities during the Lee Myung-bak regime. This was the result of the three cities' interest relationships being harmonized. The dilapidated Masan City wanted to integrate with Changwon City to gain financial support and regenerate the city. As the city of Changwon was already well developed, the financial incentive was weak but expected to develop into a mega city through integration. Finally, Jinhae City had the weakest influence among the three cities, and the Mayor of Jinhae City called for the integration of Changwon City and Jinhae City. Therefore, Jinhae City could participate in the discussion of integration.

At the beginning of the integration process, a number of combinations were presented to maximize the profits of their regions, including 'Changwon city-Massan city', 'Changwon city – Jinhae city', 'Changwon city -Masan city', and others. However, a survey conducted by the Ministry of Public Administration and Security showed that the "Changwon city-Masan city-Jinhae city" proposal had higher support. In the process, the central government emphasized the subjective aspects of local government. There were efforts and conflicts to directly reflect the opinions of citizens, such as the demand for a "referendum by 3 cities" NGO and the poll results by the Gyeongnam newspaper. Underlying factor in the conflict was competitiveness among these three cities. Finally, the Changwon integrated city was launched on July 1, 2010. Currently, this megacity has a population of 1.06 million and an annual budget of about 2.8 trillion won.

Currently, while the major regionalism of the Southeast region vs Southwest region confrontation in Korea is relatively weakening, minor-regionalism continues to happen in the region. NIMBY, representing "not in my back yard", and PIMBY, meaning "please in my back yard", are the key attitudes intensified since decentralization reforms. This is because major regionalism is now combined with the president's desire for unbalanced regional development and democratization in the process of industrialization. Still, minor-regionalism continues because it is related to the direct interests and rivalry of the local people. In particular, minor-regionalism is becoming stronger as the provinces collapse and the concentration in Seoul and the capital area intensifies. As mentioned previously, if small regionalism is not managed well, too much competition will disrupt the management of state affairs. Therefore, the central government needs to take good care of regional competitiveness.

Local economy development and policy competition

One of the regionalist behaviors is the competition for infrastructure development with neighboring rivals. The typical slogan of the electoral campaign is "if you vote for me, this region will have a railway (or highway)". When infrastructure such as railroads and roads are constructed, the economic development effect in the region will be huge, as more and more citizens will travel to the cities. Paradoxically, this is also due to the disproportionate development of the nation's territory in the capital metropolitan area and the Southeast region.

However, the rationale behind candidates' infrastructure construction pledges in local elections is often not in terms of policy, such as geographical advantage, economic effect, or budget. The basis of the pledge is often based on the candidate's relationship with the central government, the central party, or a powerful politician, rather than a reasonable policy. The cause of the problem is that the administration is too conscious of the political support of the local people. And the problem is getting worse, as each local government's attempt to somehow maximize its regional interests has worsened. A recent example of infrastructure competition is the construction of a new airport in the Yeongnam region. Originally, Yeongnam region had Kimhae International Airport, but due to limitations in its location, inconvenient transportation, and the inability to expand due to geographical factors, construction of the new airport will become a hot topic.

The candidate for the site for the construction of a new airport in the Yeongnam region was Gadeok Island and Miryang City. Busan Metropolitan City and parts of Gyeongsangnam-do supported Gadeok Island. Areas supporting Miryang City were Gyeongsangbuk-do, Daegu Metropolitan City, and Ulsan Metropolitan City. While each camp competitively offered its own reasons, the most fundamental cause was, of course, the attempt to maximize its local interests. Even after time, the two camps failed to reach an agreement, and the conflict grew more acutely.

Lee Myung-bak who was the president at the time, 2011, was the most awkward figure in this situation. The reason was that if the president Lee Myung-bak were to select one side, he could lose some of the parts of the Yeongnam region that used to remain his basis for political power. For this reason, the evaluation committee of the new airport evaluated that both areas failed, and the new airport construction project would be scrapped. Of course, the two regions did not accept the results and demanded a re-election. Then the construction of a new airport was very actively discussed again when Park Geun-hye was elected president. However, the uneasy discussion over the construction came as an unexpected result of the expansion of Kimhae Airport in 2016. Later, it was revealed that French aircraft engineering, which participated in the evaluation, stated that it was decided largely by political influence. And the expansion of the Kimhae Airport, chosen as an alternative, was impossible due to geographical limitations and airport noise problems, as has been the concern since the beginning of the discussion.

Later in the 2018 local elections, the Democratic Party won, not the ruling party, which once produced the Busan mayor, Ulsan mayor, and provincial governor of Gyeongsangnam-do. Now Moon Jae in, the current president, who belongs to the Democratic Party is pushing to build an international airport on Gadeok Island, Busan, Korea.

As such, the construction of a new airport in the Yeongnam region clearly shows the nature of competition and conflict due to small regionalism in the Yeongnam region. As competition continues without solving the problem, regional conflicts in Yeongnam are becoming more serious, even affecting the party's competition structure overall. The cause of the problem is that the administration is too conscious of the political support of the local people. And the problem is getting worse, as each local government's attempt to somehow maximize its regional interests has worsened.

Notes

1 Kim Dong-wan, 2009, Regionalism and State Space: With a Case study of South Korea, 1961–71, Doctoral Thesis at Seoul National University, 116p (in Korean).
2 Kim Dong-wan (2009), 106p–109p.
3 Park Sang-hoon, 2013, *"The Reality Created, the Regionalism in Korea, What Is the Problem and What Is Not the Problem"*, Seoul: Humanitas, 60p.
4 Park Sang-hoon, 2013, *"The Reality Created, the Regionalism in Korea, What Is the Problem and What Is Not the Problem"*, Seoul: Humanitas, 219p.

References

Choi, Y. J. (1999). *Politics of Korean Regionalism and Identity* (in Korean). Seoul: Oruem.

Kim, D. (2009). Regionalism and State Space: With a Case study of South Korea, 1961–71 (in Korean). Doctoral thesis at Seoul National University, 1–201.

Park, S. (2013). *"The Manufactured Reality, the Regionalism in Korea, What Is the Problem and What Is Not the Problem"* (in Korean). Seoul: Humanitas.

6 Competition and governance in the future

In this chapter, the effects of competition on Korean society are evaluated and the future direction for a sustainable governance is discussed. This chapter examines the meaning of competitiveness in Korea from a temporal perspective, which Chapter 5 explained it from a spatial perspective. Focusing on its usefulness and short-term as well as long-term effects, the key social issues, such as the birth-rate, trust, education, and sports, will be discussed. The main purpose of this chapter is to think about a good governance for the future.

Positive aspects of competition

Efficiency and productivity

Competitiveness has been one of the determinant factors in the developmental period in Korea. In a sense, advocates for development whose traits were highly competitive have had more access to key positions in the government than others. Leaders in these positions, including the presidents, have created competition-friendly atmospheres in society that were previously dominated by fatalism. In the early stage of economic development, which involved a major transformation from pre-modern to modern society, government policies encouraged a competitive atmosphere throughout diverse communities. The goal was to stimulate competition among the people to overcome their fatalist attitudes that had long stemmed from the class society. For example, the *Saemaul Movement* that aimed at promoting rural developments was accompanied by a "We Can Do It" slogan. Through this slogan, the Korean government hoped farmers and rural residents would compete for better development outcomes and overcome the prevalent fatalism. The government also expected both the economy and society to become more efficient in the end, as people competed to ascend the social ladder.

In order to encourage a competition-friendly atmosphere, the state must continually recall that a victory in the competition can help the people escape poverty and lower social status, which has often been faithfully accepted in pre-modern class societies. Korea's military government adopted a combating culture in the non-military war, including, but not limited to, poverty. Since the era of rapid economic growth, enormous economic and social opportunities have emerged throughout never-ending periods of development. Once the government established a competitive atmosphere, people would need to recognize that benefits from an increased income and higher social status exceed the costs for competition, such as time and tiring efforts for exam preparation and higher education levels. In other words, in the early stage of economic growth, it had been effective for the government to enforce policies that induced income increases and upward class mobility by encouraging the entire society to compete.

Once the government successfully established a competition-prone atmosphere, society was eventually captured by excessive competition in which only the winners were valued. The phenomenon almost resembles Darwin's theory in which only the fittest survive. Competitive races in diverse dimensions throughout the Korean society and have rewarded winners in both visible and non-visible ways. Such a culture has been widespread in all aspects of Korean society: in the economy, politics, education, and all other areas. As the state develops and people enjoy economic growth over time, the opportunity for socio-economic stratification is reduced, which, in turn, satisfies people's calls for equality. As discussed through Chapters 2–5, multiple levels of competitiveness in South Korea have facilitated individual development and societal growth. Competition is embedded in every aspect of Korean society, in general, increased social efficiency and productivity by motivating people to work harder and do sufficiently better than others.

The rise of civil society

Given that Korea went through the developmental state era with its powerful central government, it seems logical that less privileged citizens felt they needed to voice their rights against privileged others. Otherwise, privileged ruling elites would not give up their advantages voluntarily. Many voices have called for a democratic governance system, and this has accelerated a remarkably rapid democratization in Korea. The direct election of a president in the midst of long military regimes and impeachment of presidents are only a few preliminary examples of Korean democracy.

As explained in Chapter 5, due to strong regionalism, the Korean government has still not been successful in fully reconstructing spatially unbalanced social developments. The competitive spirit at the regional level was one of the fundamental motivations that led to two major democratic revolutions in Korea: the June Democratic Uprising in 1987 and the Candlelight Revolution in 2016. The 1987 revolution was a clear demonstration of hopes for the realization of a *textbook* popular sovereignty. People asked for a society beyond a mere resemblance of the popular sovereignty that has long prevailed through Western communities. Once people became accustomed to competition at school, work, and community and were at the same time enlightened by democracy around the world, they aspired to a more egalitarian treatment. It was more of a fight for redistribution of rights and power endowed for the elite politics than simply overturning the existent social structure.

Competing for a better status and equal treatment not only made revolutions possible but also changed the power distribution across the society. The Candlelight Revolution in 2016 was an NGO-led realization of egalitarianism against the incumbent administration's right-wing supremacy. Both 1987 and 2016 revolutions are achievements led by citizens, who struggled to overcome regionalism that has negatively affected political and social equality. Each has opened a gateway to a fair regional representation in the participatory democracy.

As the era of rapid growth nears its end, there will be more reflections on a competitive social atmosphere that has failed to respect losers in competition. A recently common observation is a social environment in which cultural diversity and personal happiness thrive with the help of democracy. This is the point where the economy achieves stability while experiencing a lower growth rate. Inter-class movements are less common, meaning that the cost of competition may exceed its benefits.

Negative aspects of competition

The wicked problem of education

The downside of competitiveness comes from the discordance of pursued social value with the present status of the country. Yet it is notable that various symptoms of South Korean society point out that competitiveness now malfunctions when applied in its old way. The individual level of education competition that used to lead to the strong human capital of South Korea now only worsens the youth problem. According to OECD statistics, South Korea's suicide rate not only has ranked at the top for 12 full years from 2003 to 2015 but also has increased rapidly. The top cause of death in the millennium generation, members of which were born from 1980–2000, is, tragically, suicide. People in their twenties die from killing themselves as often as from all other reasons (44.8%). According to Durkheim (1897), suicide is based on two dimensions which are social integration and social regulation. Psychologists accept Durkheim's theory as the proposition that suicide happens more at the social integration level (Johnson, 1965). The young generation taking their own life reflects the fact that the transmission of traditional collectivist values from the older generation has failed.

Intra-organizational competition also does not work since the traditional extended family system is now splitting in favor of the nuclear family. As discussed earlier, education competition was not only about the individual itself but about the familial desire for upward intergeneration mobility. As within-family and between-family competition is disappearing, the competitiveness that used to have an advantage when it is combined familism turned into a catalyst for social division.

This matters because South Korea now needs social capital rather than economic and human capital, which are relatively abundant. The Korean Development Institute surveyed the perception of high school to college students in four different countries, and most Korean students attested to "a battlefield of life". Meanwhile, students from China, Japan, and the United States answered "a square together" and "a battlefield of life" at almost equal proportions. Korean students perceived the circumstances dismal even among Asian countries.

Competition for the big college admissions is mainly responsible for this particular phenomenon in Korea. A college diploma is not just a certification for one's ability to achieve a certain level in a field. Rather, it works as a positional good, whose value is determined by its image rather than its function or quality. A person graduated from the top universities will be differentiated throughout his whole life from one who only has a high school diploma. A diploma mattered more than one's true ability, especially when entering the job market or being introduced to others. Parents, regardless of their level of education, have experienced the importance of a college diploma and they set their children's goals to enter a good college. Influenced by their parents and social atmosphere, children acknowledge the importance of being in college in their early days. They get involved with private tutoring aside from normal school hours. From the early days of their life, starting from 9 or 10 years old, they take private tutoring to achieve better grades than their peers.

In some schools, especially those in high-income districts, students often discriminate their friends for low grades in school exams. Sleep deprivation of adolescents then rises as a social problem. Governments have attempted reforms aiming at ensuring quality sleep and stress relief of adolescents. Local governments and the central government thus set various goals to solve these problems. For example, governments have adopted a policy to ban private tutoring after 10 PM. To reduce students' stress, the central government has even made restrictions on the difficulty level of CSAT, the national test for scholastic aptitude. Many officials attributed students' stress to CSAT because it has been too difficult for students. However, the causal relationship between the difficulty level of CSAT and students' stress level has not been statistically justified. Judging from current circumstances, while difficulty levels of CSAT have been lowered in recent years, it is hard to tell if students are freed from CSAT stress. Rather, their stress level might even have been increased. Because a college applicant no longer can sufficiently differentiate him/herself by his/her CSAT score, he/she has to prepare extra-curriculum records more thoroughly. Regardless of how much the government thrives to adjust the level of competition, it is very difficult for the government to cure the dysfunctions of competitiveness. It is hard to tell if the policy has achieved its goal because education has been a positional good for a long time in Korean society, and policy subjects thus do not comply. It is, as a matter of fact, the wicked problem of the current Korean education system (Figure 6.1).

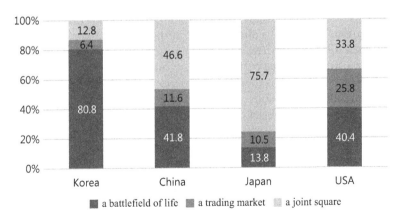

Figure 6.1 Recognition of college students from four countries for their high school's image.

Source: Author's graph drawn from Kim Hi-sam (2017).

This social disease is not a phenomenon confined to students but spread in all generations. Public health and well-being are deteriorating or, at least, not thriving much. Although life expectancy at birth has increased from 66.8 years (1985) to 82.3 years (2016), a healthy life expectancy remained stable as 64.9 years (2016) and 65.7 years (2012).[1] The wide gap between life expectancy and health expectancy signifies that people are living an unhealthy life, spending their last years in suffering. Indeed, Korea ranked the second among OECD countries, following Lithuania, in the suicide rate at 25.6% in 2017. Koreans are one of the most over-working populations in the world, ranking second out of 34 OECD countries for long working hours. Average working hours per year in Korea is 2,113 hours, much higher than Japan, where a word *karoshi*, meaning death from long hours, was invented and has become a serious social problem. The OECD released statistics in 2016 about average sleeping hours of male and female adults. The statistics revealed that Koreans spent 462 minutes on average every day, which is the second lowest amongst OECD countries, following Japan.

Social problems due to hyper-competitiveness

While Korea has achieved so many things that it had not before, such as hosting international mega-sports events (1988 and 2018), reaching 10,000 dollars GDP per capita (1995), turning from a donor country into a recipient (2009), and many other formal achievements, dysfunctions of competitiveness have often been underestimated. These days, Korea is facing a low economic growth trap, and many find themselves unemployed yet unwilling to have underpaying jobs. Compared to generations in their 50s and 60s who in their 20s had hopes that one day their life will get better, young generations have little sense of hope that their future will be better than it is today.

The growth rate is becoming lower, and previously unknown or unstated dysfunctions of competitiveness are appearing in the news. Every generation of South Korea has shown relatively low and declining general social trust in the World Values Survey for recent decades. Even though the government is taking a greater role in delivering social welfare in place of families, paradoxically, people's trust in government has been decreasing continuously. A well-designed institution is called for again. With regard to government competitiveness, a new direction toward accumulating social capital is in demand.

The low birth-rate is becoming more and more problematic. The economic growth rate may or may not depend on the birth-rate and the availability of young workers, but competition is likely to become looser than in the era of rapid economic growth. Some younger singles defy the traditional family because they do not want their children to suffer from fierce competition that the older generations have borne. Many believe that competition is becoming problematic, beyond its positive effects. This phenomenon is becoming more prevalent recently, and it may affect the long-term competitiveness of Korea.

One of the renowned reasons for avoiding marriage and the low birth-rate is the housing market competition. The Korean housing market has been overheated in the last half a decade. Because the housing price, in general, has skyrocketed in recent years, the rate of price growth has exceeded the overall price growth rate (growth rate of the consumer price index). Investment in housing has long been considered a shortcut to piling up a fortune: buy an apartment and two or three years later, make a profit far above the interest rate. This has been a formula for fortune building for middle-class families in Korea. However, once two previous administrations of President Lee and President Park have boosted housing sales through lowering interest rates for mortgages, more and more people started to enter the housing markets by speculating on higher housing prices in the near future. With demand exceeding supply in certain metropolitan areas and housing prices rising every day, newlyweds and singles have feared not being able to purchase or rent a house. Keeping housing price at an appropriate level has been one of the top priorities of every administration over the past 20 years. Governments stepped in to control the market rate of rents and price growth, but it will take time to lessen the intense competition for quality housing by increasing supply and deterring mortgages.

Another example of overheated competition is one for a public official position. Many Korean young adults spend their 20s preparing for the national exam for public positions. They consider public positions to be stable, with virtually no fear of being fired once they get in. The average competition rate hit roughly 50:1 for different types of Civil Service Exam, which means only 1 out of 50 applicants are able to pass the exams. Average months to study and pass the exam is about 52 months (in 2016). Among those who have passed the manager level public official, around 19% have prepared for the exam for more than five years. Many of the exam applicants have graduated (or are soon to be graduating) prestigious university such as Seoul National University, Korea University, Yonsei University, and so forth. It may be alright to spend their youth competing to become a public official if they ever pass the exam, but many do not. There are words for this phenomenon – a 'civil servant examination tribe' and 'gosi (short in

Korean for public official examination)-vagabond'. While preparing for the public official examination, the gosi-vagabonds usually seclude themselves from society and do not invest their time for anything else. With no success for years, they lack self-confidence and are incompetent at doing anything else than the Civil Service Exam.

Competitors seek to win in the competition not by differentiating him/herself but by following the best example or a front-runner. Without diversity in mode, a competition can become a race of time and hard work instead of a race of capability. The winner gets to survive at the expense of his/her own and his/her family member's quality of life. In the long run, dysfunction of competition stretches out to family trouble and, farther more, population problem. Because parents cannot guarantee their child a good quality of life due to severe lifelong competition, people are reluctant to have children. While there may be other reasons for the demographic cliff in Korea, one of, but not the least of, the causes of such a phenomenon is intensified competition.

Optimal competition

Competition may bring about incredible benefits, while it can also result in several disadvantages beyond optimal level. In the developmental state era, Korean government, entrepreneurs, and educators have achieved their goal: encourage people to compete. Competition in various areas led to improvements in productivity. As people observed more and more winners in different competitions, they were motivated to participate and win in a competition. However, once competitions help the society to cross the threshold to an advanced society, only a small proportion of the population may be able to compete with others. While the society as a whole has achieved vast improvements in technology, academics, and policies, further growth demands specific resources that are often restricted to exclusive groups of people. Those without enough resources may still survive, but they may experience frustration for not being able to compete against others who are already endowed with an unrivaled amount of resources. Frustration then leads to more people defining themselves as losers, with their psychological productivity declining. The society may fall into the trap of excessive competition. More people may be unhappy.

The logic of optimal competition thus involves two variables: competition (which is dependent on time) and productivity. Productivity may also correspond to people's happiness. Competition and productivity are demonstrated in an inverse U-curve (Figure 6.2).

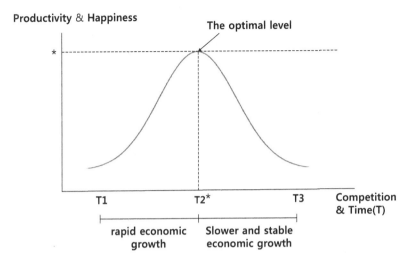

Horizontal axis: Time (t) and competition

- • t1~t2: rapid economic growth, developing state; increasing competition
- • t2: on the verge of developed state; the optimal level of competition
- • t2~t3: slower yet stable economic growth, developed state; excessive competition

Vertical axis: productivity, happiness

Figure 6.2 Competitiveness inverted U-curves.
Source: Author.

As a country enters a developed state and competition extends to a beyond-optimal level, its government should promote people's happiness. Happiness is likely to be maintained by controlling excessive competition, instead of encouraging more and more competition. In other words, the government's role should involve redistribution policies that help those in need of resources for competition. At the same time, it will no longer be the government's job to induce competition for further productivity growth. Entrepreneurs and people or the private sector should be the ones initiating growth. The government should instead enforce fair competition and help those in need to survive.

It is difficult to decide or even anticipate when the optimal level of competition will be achieved. However, given that Korea has clearly

moved on from its developmental state era, the government-led resource concentration to exclusive groups of entrepreneurs should no
longer be in effect. Also outdated is the government-led competition
that extends to every aspect of life. The government should instead
accommodate more resources for effective cooperation between
different groups of people. There are social problems that need attention from the government, as they have newly become problems.
Collectivism and familism may not be sufficient to solve the social
safety net issues in the more complex, developed state. If the government fails to pay attention to the polarized society and economy, it
will become more and more challenging to at least maintain current
accomplishments.

International competition in sports

National branding

Since the export-driven economy started, leaders realized the importance of a national image to sell goods 'made in Korea'. The Syngman
Rhee administration (1948–1960), an administration formed shortly
after restoring independence from Japanese colonial government, had
not recognized the worthiness of sports. It was not until the time of
the Park Chung-hee administration (1961–1979) that the government
started to be aware of merits of sports. President Park emphasized
the importance of physical activity with a slogan: "physical strength
is national strength". Park's administration valued sports for its instrumental merits – especially its merits for building national prestige
(Chappelet & Im, 2017). The government introduced a sports policy
specifically targeting elite athletes. The government started to award
the Order of Sports Merit and provide pensions to medalists in important international games. Athletes who performed well in international games got exempted from military service obligations. To
be accurate, the athletes served in the special military system only
for four weeks. While, generally, every man is required to serve as a
military force in their young days for over two years, the military ex-
emption was a great incentive to perform better. The Department of
Physical Education was designed in Korean universities to encourage
sports, and Tae-Rueng Athlete village was established to nurture ex-
cellent athletes as top performers.

The ultimate goal of an elite athlete who was fostered with government support was winning a prize at an international competition

like the Olympic Games. The Korean government managed the Tae-Rueng Athlete village, which nurtured national athletes through selective system to make the athletes become both competitive and active in international competitions. The Government of the Republic of Korea also provided differential support based on sports fields. They have provided much support in Ju-do, wrestling, short track, etc., which are likely to win a prize, but spent less investment in unpopular sports.

The Chun Doo-hwan administration (1980–1988), the very next administration after the Park administration, who took over by *coup d'état*, had actively used sports to stabilize society, in turn, to secure its own power. President Chun Doo-hwan unfolded a '3S policy' – where each S represents sex, screen, and sports – to redirect public attention to something other than politics (Chappelet & Im, 2017: 125). During the seven years of the Chun administration, the government successively hosted the 1988 Seoul Summer Olympics and the 1986 Asian Games. With the host of the Olympics, sports agenda intertwined with international agenda under the slogan "Seoul to the World! The World to the Seoul!" While there had been no government ministry in full charge of sports administration before the Chun administration, the Chun administration established the Ministry of Sports and often designated the presidents' most favored person as the minister. The governments' full support on sports had reached its peak when preparing for the 1988 Seoul Summer Olympics. Being a member of Organizing Committee for the 1988 Seoul Summer Olympics meant a great honor and was a great career. A lot of competent public officials wanted to contribute to organizing the Olympics, and many volunteered. In 1988, literally, almost every citizens' attention was directed toward sports and Olympics. There was this collective aspiration to present the country to the world as a competent and charming country.

Extensive investment in elite sports has come to fruition. From independence to 1972, Korea athletes never had won a gold medal in the Summer and Winter Olympics. To win a few bronze medals, silver at most, was the best record they could ever achieve. However, such limits were overcome after extensive government intervention in sports. After winning a gold medal and reaching the record total medal count (6) in 1976, performance – in terms of medal count in mega-sports events – of athletes in Korea has sprung. In 1988 Seoul Summer Olympics, Korea ranked fourth among all participating countries. Since then Korea has ranked around 5th to 12th (Figure 6.3).

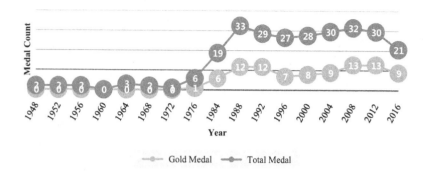

Figure 6.3 Medal count by Olympic Games.
Source: Author.

Reproducing competitiveness in international games

It had been a more efficient option for the former administrations to invest in elite sports rather than to invest in public sports. There was not enough budget to assure that every person in the country to enjoy a modest level of physical activity. For the people who were short in possession, spectating sports via media was a joyful enough activity. High performing elite sports in international games gave the people pride in their country. Thus, the Park Chung-hee administration invested in supporting high performing athletes and the Chun Doo-hwan administration invested in the successful operation of the 1988 Seoul Summer Olympics. Both the Park and Chun administrations' policy focusing on elite sports were a great success. Professional sports thrived and athletes were more competent than ever. Korean people were satisfied with their country attaining a good record in the international sports field and with their country hosting the biggest sports game in the world. The two administrations' sports policy had fulfilled the competitive nature of the people in an efficient manner. Since then, succeeding administrations' sports policies were not much different from those of the former two administrations. The government's sports policy can be abstracted into two characteristics – to win the right to host a mega international sports event and to win a prize in an international sports game.

In the 1988 Seoul Summer Olympics, where 13,600 athletes from 160 nations participated, Korea accomplished splendid record – 12 gold medals, 10 silver medals, 11 bronze medals and, in turn, ranking fourth overall. Since then, rankings and medal counts in international games have become the prime concern of the people in any international mega-sports events. When rankings and medal counts were poor, it was the government to blame. Because sports competition was driven mainly by the government, people pointed out a lack of governmental support for the low performance of sports. When, for example, Yuna Kim, a prominent figure skater, won prizes from international games, people who inspired her acknowledged how she strived to be a top figure skater despite inferior figure skating facilities compared to some Western countries, such as Canada. They criticized how much the government was indifferent to the figure skating environment. As such, the dramatic success story of an athlete impresses the people who admire him/her and, subsequently, illuminates the lack of governmental assistance. While the former two administrations, the Park administration and Chun administration, focused on elite sports for national prestige and to coordinate social conflict, the following administrations had another reason to concentrate on elite sports. It was to keep up with people's expectation and to avoid public bashing.

On the other hand, the following governments have been struggling to host international mega-sports events. A phenomenon that the fruitful accomplishments of hosting mega-sports events retain throughout people's memory and that drives politicians to pursue the hosting of future mega events can be referred to as the "trap of the Olympics" (Chappelet & Im, 2017). No one can actually be certain of what had once been success will again be successful in the future. People, however, repeatedly located mega-sports event to their regions hoping to take advantage of huge investments on infrastructure, for example. Knowing voters' sentiment of relative deprivation compared with Seoul, politicians use regionalism, i.e. trait competitiveness, by promising to host a big sports event to their region. Since then, Korea had hosted various international sports events – 2002 Korea-Japan World Cup, 2002 Busan Asian Games, 2011 Yeongam Formula One, 2011 Daegu World Championship in Athletes, 2014 Incheon Asian Games, 2018 Pyeong-Chang Winter Olympics, and so on.

Regarding the logic of public debate, one can find patterns of political games in the process of hosting these sports events (Chappelet & Im, 2017: 97–108). Before the attraction of an event, people and politicians in a candidate city anticipate great economic benefits. Some research institutions analyze the cost and benefits of hosting a game and conclude that benefits exceed costs significantly. They assess non-economic values such as personal utility and equity with high weight along into the B/C analysis. Weighting subjective values leads to over-emphasizing the benefit-side comparing to cost-side. The B/C analysis makes a great contribution to evaluate the event as eligible to host. However, the possibility of failure, that is the possibility of cost offsetting benefit, is exposed after nomination as a hosting city. City governments, which hosted a game even with the central government's opposition, claim burden sharing with the central government.

The government has devoted itself to win in international competition. While building a country brand, for some, the country may be rotting inside. Concentration on elite sports and mega-sports events made the government somewhat blind to important matters – the public health and well-being. Along with the "Sports for all" motto that prevailed in the world in the 1990s, the Government of Korea tried to invigorate public sports (Cho, 2012). Sports policy and governmental support, however, have always been centered around elite sports, not around public wellness, in spite of such an effort.

Sports competition and physical education

Focusing on elite sports through international mega-events has not been limited to people related to elite sports and government but has extended to the whole of Korean society. Especially this national policy heavily influenced children's education. The Ministry of Education, on the other hand, had built numbers of policies in school sports for meeting the national goal.

In 1971, as part of the training of elite athletes, the Department of Physical Education was established in universities to provide special education for outstanding athletes under the support of the state. The student-athletes from the school of physical education was able to win in various competitions through strong support of the government and guidance, and intensive training only in physical education subjects. The student-athlete who graduated from a school could enter the university by athlete special entrance system and became a professional player.

In addition, the government decided to evaluate the results of middle schoolers' physical fitness tests in high school entrance examinations (1972) and those of high schoolers' in university entrance examinations (1973). Since the level of education meant something prestigious in Korea and there was a heated competition over college admission, students had to show a good record in the physical fitness test. According to a newspaper article of the time, the school sports policies had some achievements – the students' attained a higher record in school physical fitness test than before the policies were implemented.[2]

However, what the administration adopted as policies of school sports were either short-sighted or partial. By short-sighted, we mean that the outputs of physical activity did not last long. Although the purpose of physical fitness tests was to promote national physical activity, the effects of such policy did not have a chance for a continuous improvement of physical strength of the people. Instead, it accomplished only a small rise in student records between high school entrance examination and college entrance examination. By partial, we mean school sports policies were only a part of elite sports policies. The Park administration provided special discipline to outstanding athletes in schools and allowed sports talents to enter college through an athlete special admission route. Such policies might be classified as a school policy but, nevertheless, they only exist to promote elite athletes.

Park Chung-hee emphasized physical education under the slogan "Physical strength is national strength". In order to disseminate and develop government physical education, two competition induction policies were used (Chappelet & Im, 2017: 129–131). One is that the government reflected the result of the physical fitness test system for the promotion of national physical education to the high school entrance examination in 1972, and to the school entrance examinations sequentially in the university entrance examination in 1973. Korea had educational fever and going to a prestigious school was a very important issue for students. In this situation, physical fitness was reflected as an element of the college entrance examination, which caused competition in physical education.

In order to measure the physical fitness of the students, the Park Chung-hee government selected eight sports, such as long-running, chin-ups, throwing, and long jump, and divided these into six grades. And when the quantitative indicators through these physical fitness tests were reflected in each school entrance examination, the students began to pay attention to the result of the physical fitness test to go to a good school. According to an article on November 18, 1972, in the Dong-A Ilbo,[3] the result of the physical test showed that the number of top grades that were not even male and female in March increased by 23.7% for male students and 11.2% for female students. It is said that the starting physical fitness test proved to be effective in improving the physical fitness of middle school students. This means that physical education policy using competition for entrance was effective in improving students' short-term physical strength.

However, side effects also existed. Unlike the purpose of the physical fitness test, which is the promotion of the national physical strength, the physical activity is concentrated only during the physical fitness test. And because there was no physical activity between the high school entrance examination and the college entrance examination, the physical fitness system did not lead to continued enjoyment of sports for the rest of the peoples' lives. It was the limit of excessive competition for the entrance examination.

How to rectify

Why do nations intervene in sports? One might answer that such an intervention results from an aim for individual well-being and preservation of health. Surely, the wellness and well-being of an individual are the prime goal of sports. However, to improve the level of wellness and well-being by a means of sports demands a great deal of support and care, and is an extremely long shot. Sports have been valued more for other functions than a function of wellness and well-being – from a nations' standpoint, sports are a priceless tool to enhance national prestige, to manage social conflict, to flourish economic growth, and to deal with foreign countries in a peaceful manner. Prime value of sports in a viewpoint of government was more instrumental than intrinsic, especially it has been a case in Korea.

Being competitive and being competent are two different things. To this day, however, competitiveness contributed to being competent. Take medal counts in the Summer Olympics for example. Korea had been competitive over international sports performance and its ambition had its fruits. Sports in Korea have grown in quantity, claiming to be one of the top-rank countries in elite sporting events. And yet, one cannot help asking the question: winning competition over elite sporting events. Despite enrapturing scores in elite sports, average people live a long but unhealthy life. Considering the people sleeping less, working more and, presumably, exercising less, is a good record in elite sports worthwhile? Unlike the old days, competitiveness in sports does not fully transfer into competence. Now that well-being is recognized as a value to achieve with governmental intervention, it is better to encourage a new spirit of community rather than to promote competitiveness.

Concluding remark

Korean society has achieved significant developments in both its economy and politics thanks to the high competitiveness. Thus, the role of government to instigate competition between the members of a society was elaborated on. The Korean government not only takes initiatives in policy areas by direct intervention but also encourages a competition-friendly atmosphere throughout its communities. Such actions differ from the more traditional institution-building nature of a government.

However, making a more competitive society is not the panacea to cure all social diseases let alone the problem of underdevelopment. To the contrary, it can be a cause of governance problems. Korean cases have shown that competition has become extremely fierce in many areas of society. Competition beyond an optimal level has led to social stress and even inefficiencies. Competition has often destroyed social capital: from families, which have been said to be the most preliminary sources of competition, to friendships, entrepreneurs, and governments. The current governance is at risk in this regard.

A sustainable governance can be realized if the competitive level remains under the optimal level of a society. Korean society needs to change the dominant paradigm focusing on economic success to a new, sustainable one. Someone should raise question about "why should we be competitive for a long run?" A good governance is the collective way of assuring how people live in a happy and healthy life. The need for an optimal level of competition could not be more stressed.

Notes

1 http://www.index.go.kr/potal/main/EachDtlPageDetail.do?idx_cd=2758.
2 Dong-A Ilbo. Performance of school physical fitness test (November 18, 1972).
3 Ibid.

References

Chappelet, J. L., & Im, T. (2017). *Physical Education Governance for Successful Olympic Games* (in Korean). Seoul: Danhanmedia.

Cho, W. Y. (2012). International comparative study on sports for all policy patterns. *Journal of the Korea Contents Association*, 12(4), 457–467.

Durkheim, E. (1897). *Suicide: A Study in Sociology*. New York: The Free Press.

Johnson, B. D. (1965). Durkheim's one cause of suicide. *American Sociological Review*, 30, 875–886.

Kim, Hi. S. (2017). *The Role of Education in Social Capital and Policy Directions* (in Korean). Seoul: KDI.

Kim, M. J. (2017). The aspects of 1970s physical education policy by reviewing the physical fitness tests (in Korean). *The History Education Review*, 25, 43–74.

Index

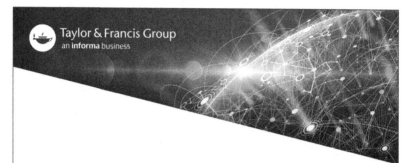

Printed in the United States
by Baker & Taylor Publisher Services